I0567664

MY PAIN IS MY IDENTITY

Lawyer Johnson

The story in this book reflects the author's recollection of events. Names, locations, and identifying characteristics have been changed to protect the privacy of those depicted. The dialogue has been re-created from memory. All events occurred and have not been fabricated.

Copyright © 2025 by: Lawyer Johnson

Table of Contents

PROLOGUE

It was a summer morning. I was seven years old.

My neighbor—a man I trusted—offered me cookies if I'd help him move something in his basement. With the innocence only a child could have, I followed him downstairs.

That moment—just one decision, made without hesitation—became the invisible line that split my life in two: *before* and *after*.

Before that day, I was a joyful boy who idolized Michael Jackson and dreamed of becoming a firefighter, maybe even a soldier. I believed the world was good, that people were kind, and that I was safe. But after? After, I became something else—suspicious, angry, broken, and self-destructive. What happened in that basement didn't just take something from me—it changed who I was at my core. And it would take over forty years to fully understand how those moments set me on a path from Green Acres housing projects to Rikers Island, from childhood trauma to incarceration, from breaking out of jail to breaking generational curses.

This is the story of what was stolen from me… of what I stole from others. But more than that, it's the story of how I reclaimed my soul—and how I now help others reclaim theirs.

To understand the weight of what I lost, you first have to know who I was before.

Before the Basement

Before everything changed, my life was made up of small joys. Saturday mornings were the best: no school, cartoons on the TV, and a pantry full of cereal my mom kept stocked just for us. She was the queen of snacks—frozen pot pies, pizzas, TV dinners, Wonder Bread with peanut butter and jelly. My sisters, Gigi and Sarah, would fight over the sticker that came in the bread bag while I lounged in front of the TV, watching *Space Ghost* and *Justice League*, waiting for my friends to come outside to play.

Gigi, my big sister, was always four years ahead of me in everything—life, fashion, attitude—but no matter how cool she got, she never stopped looking out for me. We had a bond rooted in respect and love. I learned a lot just by watching how our mother raised her. She'd roll her eyes at being asked to walk Sarah and me to the store, too embarrassed to be seen as a babysitter, but she did it anyway. Gigi had swag—Lee and Levi jeans, colorful Izod shirts. And sometimes, I'd sneak into her closet and "borrow" them. She wasn't thrilled when I got grass stains on her Levi's, but that didn't stop me.

There was one time Mom sent Gigi to the mall with money to buy clothes for all of us. I saw a pair of Nikes I wanted more than anything, but they were expensive. I begged. She hesitated, then gave in. I asked her what she'd tell Mom when she noticed the missing money. She looked at me and said, "Don't worry about it. I'll make up an excuse." That was Gigi—protective, cool, selfless.

And then there was Sarah. If Gigi was the cool older sister, Sarah was the warrior. She never backed down from anything. My mom used to joke that she must have dropped Sarah on her head as a baby because she was wild. But to me, she was just fearless. She was loyal, she was funny, and she was my protector. I never doubted she had my back.

Sarah was the kind of sister who would jump into a fight I was already winning, just to make sure. Her favorite move? Biting. One time, she sank her teeth into a kid's back who was messing with me. He ran home crying. That's who Sarah was—ride or die.

When I cut my leg on a busted bike frame and had to get stitches, Sarah was right there beside me in the emergency room. When the doctor gave me a numbing shot and I cried out, I heard her yelling from the hallway, "Don't be hurting my brother!"

We lived on North Miller Street, where kids of all ages played together. Terrance, my best friend since I was two, lived in the same building. We idolized the Jackson Five, especially Michael. My mom had every one of their albums. When "Ben" came out, we played it until the record cracked.

Being the baby of the family had its perks. When Stretch Armstrong hit the shelves, I had one. When I was into war movies, Mom bought me green Army men, tanks, walkie-talkies—you name it. When Reggie Jackson was big, she got me his candy bars, the bat, the helmet. My birthday cakes were always decked out with whatever I loved that year. One had a giant football on it that said, "Happy Birthday, Lawyer!"

What made my childhood even sweeter was having my cousins close by. My Aunt D.—Mom's older sister—had four kids: Remi, Todd, Tanisha, and Natasha. Holidays were spent at their house, packed with laughter and dance battles. Easter was my favorite. Aunt D. and Mom would dye eggs and hide them around the house. And Uncle F., My Aunt D.'s husband, had a basement workshop with a foosball table and enough space for us to ride Big Wheels around in circles.

We had each other's backs. If one cousin had beef, the whole crew got involved. One time, Todd got into a fight with a kid named Sammy. We all jumped in. During the chaos, I bit someone's leg—

only to find out it was Todd's. Sarah had already sunk her teeth into Sammy. Tanisha covered for me, saying, "Lawyer was just trying to help. They had on the same pants!"

Tanisha was tough. She didn't take crap from anyone. One time we were racing down a hill, and she fell and got the wind knocked out of her. I panicked because I thought she was dying. I'd seen mouth-to-mouth on TV, so I tried it. She came to, cursed me out, and we've laughed about it ever since.

When my mom had to be hospitalized, I stayed with Aunt D. and Uncle F. I hated it. Aunt D. was strict; no junk food, no colorful cereals. I wasn't allowed to leave the table until I finished my bland oatmeal. I missed my mom desperately.

Then came the moment I snapped.

We were watching TV, and Todd was sprawled out on the floor. I was so full of anger and frustration from missing my mom that I stabbed him in the butt with a giant safety pin. He screamed, ran to my Uncle F., and I got the beating of my life and was locked in a dark room. But I didn't care. I just wanted my mother.

When she finally came home, I wouldn't let go of her hand. The world was right again. She didn't even unpack before cooking our favorite meal.

Those were the last pure moments of my childhood. Before fear. Before shame. Before silence.

Before…… the basement.

My mother was, and will always be, my hero. Her strength and sacrifice filled our home with everything we needed—warmth, food, and unconditional love. But even with her unwavering presence, there was still a missing piece in our family picture. A silence that echoed louder the older I got.

It was the absence of my father.

I never met him. Never saw a picture. But that didn't stop me from wondering. From asking. From dreaming.

"Where's my dad?"

"What does he look like?"

"What's his name?"

Every time I asked, my mother gave me the same calm, steady answers. "His name is Smitty. He looked like Richard Roundtree. Handsome man." She'd smile gently, like she was trying to protect me from a truth too heavy for a child to carry. Maybe she thought that if she painted him in a good light, it would help me feel less abandoned.

But the truth lingered in the silence between us.

He wasn't there and that void felt massive, especially when I'd see my friends with their dads or even just a grandfather picking them up after school. I had no grandfathers. Both were gone before I could form memories. There was no man in my life I could look to and say, *That's who I'll grow up to be.*

And still, I held out hope.

Sometimes, when I'd burst into our apartment after playing outside, sweaty and tired, I'd find a man sitting with my mother. A stranger. One wore binoculars around his neck. I didn't know who he was, but I asked him all about them. He let me look through them for a minute before Mom ushered him into the bedroom. I wondered, *could that be my father?* I never asked. I was too afraid of the answer. So I carried the questions quietly.

In those moments, I built a version of my father in my mind—a perfect man. Strong, cool, loving. He wore nice clothes, had a slick car, and wore jewelry like the men on TV. He'd toss a football with me, teach me how to ride a bike, show up at my school plays, and tell me he was proud. He was everything I needed him to be—because I had nothing else to hold onto.

At night, I'd lie in bed and imagine him coming to rescue me, especially after the abuse. I imagined him bursting through that basement door, face twisted in rage, fists flying, grabbing that sick man and beating the life out of him. He'd turn to me and say, "You're safe now. No one will ever touch you again." And I would believe him.

That fantasy played on a loop in my head for years. It was both a comfort and a curse. Because when I opened my eyes, reality reminded me: no one came.

The pain of his absence grew heavier with time. It became a part of me—a quiet ache that never left. And it taught me something dangerous: not to expect protection. Not to believe in safety. And worst of all, not to speak my truth.

Because when that neighbor hurt me, I told no one.

My mother noticed something was off. She'd ask, "Why don't you want to play outside anymore?" Or "Why are you always hanging around me?" I didn't have the words. I didn't have the courage. I just said, "I want to be with you." But what I meant was: *I'm scared. I don't feel safe out there. That man is still out there.*

But I couldn't say it. I was afraid she wouldn't believe me. Or worse, that she'd be disappointed. The shame I carried wasn't mine to hold, but I didn't know that then. I thought staying silent would keep me safe.

So I did what a lot of abused children do: I buried it.

I smiled when I had to and laughed when it was expected. But my spirit was breaking. The world that had once felt warm and fun now felt threatening. I stayed close to my sisters. I stayed close to the building. I wouldn't go anywhere alone—not even to walk home from my aunt's house.

Gigi would say, "You've walked home by yourself a hundred times before, what's wrong now?" But I couldn't explain. I was too ashamed. Too scared. The threat wasn't just physical—it was psychological. That man's warning echoed in my head every day: *Don't say anything.*

And so I didn't.

Instead, I prayed. Every night, I asked God to get us out of that place. I didn't care where—just far away. I prayed for a miracle.

And one day, it came.

My mother told us we were moving to North Carolina. I still remember the feeling in my chest— like I could finally breathe. My cousins were heartbroken, but I felt relief. A chance to leave the block. The building. *Him.*

My mother's friend, whose family owned a store in our neighborhood, offered us a ride. They had family in North Carolina, too. We sold everything. Our apartment was stripped bare. On the day we left, it was raining. My mother stopped at Jack in the Box to buy food for my cousins. We didn't get out of the car to say goodbye, but the look on their faces said everything.

It was around 1 p.m. when we pulled away from Newburgh. I sat in the back seat, watching the city fade, watching the trees blur past the window. As

night fell and morning rose again, I saw it—
Welcome to North Carolina.

To the outside world, it was just a move.

But to me, it was salvation.

Chapter 1

THE MOVE

In 1980, my family and I left Newburgh, New York, and headed south to begin a new life in Goldsboro, North Carolina. I was 9 years old. My sister Sarah was 10. Gigi was 13. And my mother—just 30 years old at the time—was carrying the weight of the world on her shoulders, doing everything she could to guide her children to a better future.

We arrived in Goldsboro with tired eyes, heavy hearts, and the last of our belongings packed into the backseat. Life as we knew it had been left behind. Now, the unfamiliar southern air, thick with humidity and the scent of red clay, marked the beginning of a new chapter. A chapter we didn't ask for, but one we were determined to survive.

We pulled up to my Aunt V.'s house. She lived in a section of Goldsboro known as West Haven, a housing project community where survival and strength were stitched into the fabric of daily life. Aunt V. was my great aunt—the younger sister of my late grandmother—and the rock we clung to as my mother tried to regain her footing. We stayed with her until my mother secured an apartment of our own, but those first few weeks under her roof left a lasting imprint on me.

Aunt V. was one of those rare souls built of grit and grace. She had a no-nonsense way about her, but it was wrapped in the kind of love that only came from deep roots and hard lessons. She had a heart of gold and a work ethic unmatched. She didn't just welcome us into her home—she folded us into her rhythm of life. Her voice, strong and warm, delivered stories that were equal parts wisdom and history—tales of sharecropping, of farm life, of family legacies passed down through sweat and struggle.

She believed in family, in structure, and in instilling values that would last far beyond her years. If it weren't for her steady hand, my mother might not have made it through the overwhelming transition from New York to the rural South. And if it weren't for her generosity, I wouldn't be the man I am today.

Aunt V. had five children: Lance, Roland, James, Petunia, and Bernice. All but Bernice were closer to my mother's age. Bernice, with her kind spirit and unshakable strength, was closest to my sister Sarah in age, and quickly became one of our safe spaces. She had a smile that made you feel welcome, an honesty that commanded respect, and a generosity that made her unforgettable. I admired the way she carried herself—confident, grounded, always ready to help. She became more like a cousin than a distant relative.

The South was different. Everything moved slower, spoke louder, and meant more. The culture shock hit me like a brick wall. Back in New York, life moved fast and was full of rhythm and expression. Down here, life revolved around church, tradition, and humility. The values in North Carolina ran deep: respect your elders, say "yes ma'am" and "no sir," never talk back, and always, always give back. These lessons didn't come from a school—they came from Aunt V., from Bernice, from the land itself.

And speaking of land—our first summer was a crash course in hard labor.

We were up by 4 a.m., dressed and out the door by 5. By 6:30, we were standing in endless rows of cucumber fields, shoulder to shoulder with my mother, Aunt V., Bernice, and my siblings—each of us armed with a five-gallon bucket and the determination to earn our fifty cents per fill. Two full buckets dumped into a sack earned us a dollar. It wasn't glamorous. It wasn't easy. The sun punished us. The bugs tormented us. The dirt clung to our skin like second skin. For my mother and Aunt V., this was just another day's work. For the rest of us? It was misery. Still, I followed my mother's lead, learning how to pick the best cucumbers, how to move fast, how to endure.

Our only break was from 12 to 1, and the work didn't stop until 4 p.m. But no matter how hard it got, those days taught me more about resilience and family than any classroom ever could.

Living conditions were rough. Compared to New York, this was a step down. Back home, we had space. We had our own rooms, the best snacks, and a sense of independence. In West Haven, we were crammed into a single bedroom, sharing a kitchen and bathroom with my aunt's family. Privacy was a luxury we couldn't afford. Every dollar my mother earned went toward food, rent, and secondhand clothes from the Salvation Army. I went from wearing Pro-Keds to Cougars. Haircuts were few and far between. School was awkward. I was the "new kid," and worse—I felt like I didn't belong. My cousins were 700 miles away. I missed them fiercely.

The trauma from Newburgh didn't stay behind—it followed me like a ghost.

There was a neighbor in our new community who kept asking me to come rake his leaves. At first, it seemed harmless. But his approach—the tone of his voice, the way he watched me—triggered something dark. It reminded me too much of him. The predator I never told anyone about. My heart pounded in my chest. I shut it down fast, told him to leave me alone, and never went near him again. I didn't need to think. My body remembered. That old survival switch flipped, and I knew better than to let my guard down.

Eventually, my mother applied for housing assistance, and when a spot opened up, we moved to William Street. Life still wasn't glamorous, but it was a step toward stability. That's when I met Amos—my next-door neighbor. He changed everything.

Amos was three years older than I, tall, full of energy, and loved the outdoors. He was all about adventures and mischief—the kind of kid who could make climbing a tree feel like discovering a new planet. He took me under his wing like a little brother and showed me what life in North Carolina was all about. He wasn't just a friend—he was a protector. One time, older boys tried to jump us. Amos stood his ground, never flinched, and dared them to try. They backed down.

That was Amos. Brave. Fierce. Loyal. He had a Bruce Lee obsession and probably watched *Game of Death* a thousand times, mimicking the moves like he was training for a real showdown. He taught me things I didn't know, helped me feel like I had a place here. He made me believe I could belong.

William Street itself was full of kind-hearted folks. But one man stood out: our landlord, Bud.

Bud was a legend. Painter, plumber, carpenter, handyman, karate expert—he did it all. He wore a cap turned backward, kept a pencil tucked behind his ear, and carried himself with the cool confidence of Rollo from *Sanford and Son*. Bud didn't treat us like tenants. He treated us like family. He introduced us to his mother, Ms. A.—a saint of a woman. Sweet, humble, and generous beyond belief. She became my mother's closest friend. If we needed something, she found a way to get it.

When it was time to move into the housing projects, Ms. A. and Aunt V. were right there, helping Mom get utilities turned on, bringing over curtains, pots, food, and anything else they thought we might need. We had no furniture. No beds. Bud brought everything we needed—beds, couches, tables—free of charge. "Just until you get on your feet," he said. And he meant it.

God had placed these people in our lives at the exact moment we needed them. Without their help, we would've been sleeping on the floor. They didn't just give us material things—they gave us dignity. Stability. Community. Hope.

And after everything we'd been through, that kind of love? That kind of generosity?

It meant the world.

Chapter 2

THE GREEN ACRES CREW

The day finally came for us to move into public housing, and we were excited! All I could think about was having my own room and a place to call home. I went across the street to share the good news with Amos. He was sad I was leaving, but he wished my family and me the best of luck.

After saying our goodbyes, we piled into Ms. A's car and we were on our way! All I could remember was being happy, but most of all, overwhelmed when we finally reached Green Acres. The place looked like a miniature city, with all the lights and buildings as far as the eye could see. People were walking around, and I could hear children playing in the distance. What I liked most about being in Green Acres was that everything was within walking distance: the store, the Laundromat, and the basketball court. Most of my classmates lived in Green Acres or neighboring projects called Seymour Johnson, so there was always something to do. My sisters and I were happy for the first time in a long time.

Being in a new environment was exciting, but there were rules in Green Acres and an imaginary line that you didn't cross as a kid. Rule number one: if you stayed in the front of the projects (where we did), you didn't go to the back unless there was a legitimate reason for you to do so. Rule number two: you didn't associate with anyone from Seymour Johnson. For the longest time, I never knew what the back of Green Acres looked like, but I heard the wild stories of the families that pretty much controlled it. The Anderson family was the dominant force, and the Lincoln family followed. And if you had a problem with one member, the chances were that their whole family would show up at your doorstep.

The Andersons were a mean bunch with an older brother named Black, who everyone was terrified of. He was short, stocky, and darker than asphalt, but could fight. The Lincoln Family had fraternal twins named Jack and Jill. They were about 5'9" in 5th grade and skilled fighters. Once, I watched Jack choke out my friend for talking too much. That incident woke me up, and I steered clear of them afterward. I kept my head down and became part of their culture, which focused on football, gymnastics, and toughness. Anyone outside these guidelines was considered soft and got picked on. Luckily, I was a die-hard football fan who emulated the likes of Mean Joe Greene, Ed "Too Tall" Jones, and Jack Lambert. These legends were gritty, and I couldn't wait to use their moves on the football field.

I loved Green Acres because most of my friends played football, including my neighbors, Greenwood and Mark. We were all around the same age and went everywhere together. Mark and I were ten, and Greenwood was eight. Greenwood was one of the most talented kids at his age that I had ever seen. He wasn't scared to line up at running back with children five years his senior. Greenwood had good vision, was fast, and once he hit the open field, there was no catching him. Mark was a freak of nature. He reminded me of Mike

Singletary, just flat out fearless. Mark would hit people so hard that snot would fly out of their noses. When you ran up against him, you might get clotheslined into a ditch or get the wind knocked out of you.

Mark and I played recreational football together for two years and wreaked havoc on the opposing teams. We welcomed the roughness of football and never flinched when opposing teams matched our energy. Every football season, we watched games from sunrise to sundown, even breaking curfew to watch Monday Night Football. Our love for the sport was on a different level.

Mark was my brother as well as Greenwood. Greenwood actually stayed beside me, and that's why we became so close. His parents were very fond of me and treated me like their older son. Mrs. Elaine and Greenwood's father, Fred, were very intriguing to me because everybody respected them, and they lived their life to the fullest. They played music, drank beer, and smoked weed. Mrs. Elaine reminded me of Della Reese in Harlem

Nights. She was sweet, talked junk, and could back it up.

One time, she and Fred got into a fight, and she stabbed him with a butcher knife. Fred went to the hospital, and hours later, they were back together like nothing ever happened. One time, some older guys in the neighborhood tried to throw me in a ditch filled with water, and Elaine came to my rescue. Those guys never bothered me again. Fred, on the other hand, was different. He would occasionally take Greenwood and me hunting in the nearby woods. He would brief us before hunting, instructing us not to clown around and to walk with extreme caution, as he would be shooting birds and squirrels. At first, it was exciting, then I started feeling bad for the dead animals. I just couldn't understand why someone would kill an innocent animal without the intention of eating it. Mark, on the other hand, reminded me of a blue-collar worker—there wasn't a soft bone in his body. He played and fought hard. He was basically raised by his mother and his older sister, who was no joke.

In the summertime, we would catch frogs, peek through women's windows, and do odd jobs for people to make money. One time, our curiosity got the best of us, and we poured brake fluid into one of the housing authority's pickup trucks. We got caught by one of the maintenance guys. The office manager was furious and threatened to evict my mother if the engine locked up because of the brake fluid. Luckily, my mom had a friend who knew a mechanic in our neighborhood. They dropped the tank and inspected it free of cost. Mark and I were so relieved that we took a victory lap around the front of Green Acres.

After that incident, Mark and I stuck to the basics and put a lid on our crazy ideas. If it wasn't about football or listening to "Daryl Hall & John Oates," we wouldn't have anything to do with it. Mark and I were so far removed from all that trouble that the office manager offered me a job for $30.00 per month for locking and cleaning the laundromat. Back in those days, that was a lot of money. I got paid every first of the month and felt like a king when that check was cashed. Mark and I were like kids in a candy store. We bought sodas, ice cream, hot dogs, and ninja stars from our local pawn shop. We were living the dream for months until I got fired for not locking and cleaning up the laundromat on time, and I deserved it.

During this time of my childhood, everything was about laughter and getting grass stains in my pants from football. And in the summer, we would play red light, green light, and hide and go get with the girls in our neighborhood. Mark and I became very close over the years and had a mutual respect because of our backgrounds. We both grew up without fathers and were raised by single mothers on public assistance. And the closest thing to a male figure we had in our lives at the time was a hustler named Smooth, who had a lot of love for Mark and I.

He'd have us do odd jobs around his house, take us to McDonald's, and give us money, always pressing us about getting good grades and staying out of trouble. Smooth was our dude! Handsome, well-dressed, living like a movie star with flawless, model-like women. He owned the first waterbed, fish tank, dual VCRs, and premium sound system we'd seen. Only Mark and I were allowed in his house. Smooth's fashion was impeccable—linen, Italian shoes, Izod shirts, and gold medallions matching his gold-framed glasses. He was our neighborhood superstar.

One day, the cops busted his apartment door down for selling marijuana, and all of Green Acres was in an uproar. When they finally took Smooth away, he came out with one pant leg rolled up, a swinging medallion, and a Kangol hat on his head. Mark and I talked about that for days on how cool Smooth was. Eventually, Smooth would have to serve time on work release, but when his time was up, he was back on top.

Mark and I remained friends for the next two years, and he eventually moved to another housing project across town. Soon after Mark's departure, I had the privilege of meeting two new friends,

Justin and Omar. Justin stayed in my building, and Omar stayed in the building next to mine. Omar was laid back, soft spoken, and reminded me of Charlie Brown. If there was mischief around the corner, he didn't want any part of it. He was the only person I knew growing up who had a duck as a pet and thought rutabagas were delicious. Justin was vocal, spoke his mind, and didn't back down from anything. He was always talking junk! Then there was Little Larry. He was a die-hard Cowboys fan and an exceptional athlete who was good at football and basketball. Larry showed me a world outside of Green Acres. He took me to the recreational center in Webtown and taught me how to shoot pool and basketball.

One year, Larry encouraged me to sign up for recreational football for a youth league, and they ended up placing Larry, Mark, and me on the same team. A guy named Flip, who lived in my housing projects, also joined. Everybody was scared of Flip, including me! Flip became my friend and bridge to the back of Green Acres. With him co-signing me, people left me alone.

Green Acres was a world within itself. We played hard and were active in everything we did. Coming in second place wasn't an option to us; it was first place or nothing. Everyone in my housing project was like that, and we took pride in being the best. We even had rules that if you were from Green Acres, you couldn't play with the children from Seymour Johnson, which was hard for Little Larry and I to do.

Over the years, Larry and I cultivated a good relationship with our classmates who lived in Seymour Johnson, and we caught flak for it. I couldn't understand what the big deal was, since our projects were divided by fifty yards. I enjoyed being around my friends from Seymour because they were more adventurous and knew every path and fishing spot in our nearby woods. Seymour Johnson was a newer project and was more attractive than Green Acres. My Friday nights were always exciting when I hung out with my friends from Seymour. We would go to Waco, which was a Drive-In theater that showed "adult videos". We would lie between the bushes outside and watch for hours until the security guards came along and chased us away.

Back then, we didn't have a care in the world, we rolled in packs and stayed tight.

My Seymour friends consisted of Craig, Rondo, Brad, and Slim. We shared clothes and shoes, slept over at each other's houses, worked in the fields in the summertime, and rode our bikes for miles together. Little Larry was the one who introduced me to Rondo and his three siblings (Paula, Brad, and Craig). Rondo was affiliated with Seymour Johnson because his grandmother lived there. However at the time, Rondo and I both lived in the 1800 building—he was upstairs, and I was downstairs. We became close because I used to cut Mr. Smith's hair, Rondo's mother's boyfriend, for a dollar every week. That was my side hustle, and I was proud of it. We went to the same school and rolled with the same crew. All of us hung out together, played football, rode bikes, and just lived life as tight-knit kids from the same projects.

And Brad, Rondo's youngest brother, was more than just the baby of the family; he was the heart of our crew. Everyone treated him like their own little brother, and with good reason. Brad exuded a mix of innocence and street smarts that made him both endearing and reliable.

From the start, Brad and I shared a bond built on loyalty, respect, and genuine love. During our school Christmas breaks, when we had no money to buy gifts for our mothers, Brad and I would borrow his grandmother's rake and head out of Green Acres into the nicer neighborhoods to rake leaves. We'd start our day at 8 a.m. and wouldn't come back until 4 p.m. Some days, we would just make $5, but one morning, we stumbled into a blessing. A lady named Mrs. Stevenson paid us twenty bucks for her lawn. She even invited us into her home for breakfast, fixing us eggs, bacon, grits, and biscuits that were finger-licking good. Mrs. Stevenson had a heart of gold, and her daughter was my classmate. I felt so embarrassed sitting at her table pigging out, but Mrs. Stevenson made her son and daughter come greet us, and everything felt normal. That moment in my life was pivotal and emotional. I couldn't believe a stranger would invite two unknown children into her home, feed them, and pay them. I still hold that act of kindness and love close to my heart.

After we left Mrs. Stevenson's house, Brad couldn't stop talking about those biscuits and how nice her house was. Brad was like my little brother, and we cultivated a bond that would last forever.

For some reason, my Seymour friends were more genuine in their love for me. Craig, Rondo's older brother, was the oldest of my friends but was the big brother to all of us. He knew how to fix bikes, and everyone in Seymour brought theirs to him. If my bike broke, he would scold me for five minutes, but still made time to repair the issue. We all looked up to Craig because he did everything right. He never ran from a fight or backed down. He kept us in line but was always the levelheaded one in our crew. I was very fortunate to be blessed with friends like Craig and Brad. We did everything together—riding the bus, eating in the cafeteria, and fighting anyone who threatened our crew.

Chapter 3

JUNIOR HIGH SCHOOL

After settling into Green Acres and building new friendships, life started to feel a little more stable. Sarah had her group, and Gigi—well, Gigi was in love and off doing her own thing. She barely came home, often sneaking out to meet her boyfriend. Her go-to spot was the rec center—the same place Little Larry took me to play basketball. It was the social hub for popular kids her age.

This was a confusing time for me. Gigi was beginning to rebel against my mother, who was strict and believed in discipline without hesitation. Though her love was unwavering, Mom didn't believe in repeating herself. If you messed up, you got a beating—and she didn't discriminate on what she used. Weather strips, belts, switches, even her hands. She would yell, "I'm not your play toy!" as the punishment came down. Sarah and I learned quickly—don't talk back and don't miss curfew.

But Gigi wasn't having it. She kept choosing her boyfriend over boundaries.

One night, Gigi stayed out past midnight. Mom sent Sarah and me to bring her back, but Gigi refused. So, Mom threw on her slippers, marched over to where Gigi was playing double Dutch, and whooped her in front of everyone. I couldn't help but laugh—we warned her.

Despite her rebellious streak, Gigi and I were tight. She always looked out for me. When she got her own apartment, Sarah and I raided her stash of Little Debbies and cereal we never had at home. I even figured out how to sneak into her place without her knowing to grab snacks. One day, she caught me in her room with a girl on her bed. She flipped out and demanded to know how I got in. I confessed, and though she was upset, she kept my secret.

Our relationship wasn't just about what I could take from her. When I bought my first car in high school, Gigi helped me pay for gas and the balance. Later, she told me, "I knew you were serious. You bought a car before I did—and I'm older!" She always respected my hustle. But back then, I was just a sixth grader trying to find my place while watching my sister test the limits I wasn't brave enough to touch.

My daily routine was simple: go to school, come home, play until the streetlights came on. Sixth grade was about cracking jokes, breakdancing, having crushes, and learning computers—Texas Instruments, specifically. Our teachers were kind, always encouraging us with candy and affirmations. I had a learning disability, and most of my classes were in Special Ed, but I never felt like an outsider thanks to Ms. Deloris.

Ms. Deloris was a gem. She'd stay after school with me, helping me work through my assignments. She pushed me, protected me, and taught me how to read better and tackle math. She never gave up on a single student. Ms. Deloris and I would sit down for hours at her desk, going over math problems and reading assignments, which made me a better reader and problem solver. She never left a child behind because she truly loved her students.

When I moved up to seventh grade in 1983, I was 12 years old, and it felt like I lost my anchor. Ms. Deloris was gone. I still remember my last day of sixth grade—our year-end party, my bittersweet goodbye, and the long bus ride home. But there wasn't much time to dwell; summer was the work season.

Rondo and I worked ourselves to the bone every summer just to afford clothes for school. Five days a week, we picked cucumbers, string beans, and cropped tobacco. The heat was brutal. Some days, we barely made $20. My mother made sure I stayed safe—telling me to drink water, wear a hat, and take breaks. Rondo and I pushed each other. If he picked twenty buckets, I had to top him.

We chased the money, even trying harder jobs like hanging tobacco. It paid more, but it was hell. Heavy racks, hot barns, non-stop work. Weekends were our only break, and we usually just slept them away.

Junior high felt like leveling up. Craig warned us about the initiation and told us to stick together. Rondo, Flip, and I took it seriously. By summer's end, we were ready—fresh clothes, new kicks, and the confidence to walk through those doors.

Run-DMC ruled the world. Their influence was everywhere—Adidas, Kangol hats, gold chains. I wanted to be like them. I even "borrowed" clothes from Gigi's boyfriend to stay fly.

The night before school, I could barely sleep. But that morning, I was up early. Showered, dressed, sprayed down in cologne, and out the door to meet Rondo and the crew. We had a game plan: where to meet, what routes to walk, and how to move.

The first day was orientation. Six classes, seven minutes between each. One tardy got you a warning—after that, it was punishment. Paddlings or in-school suspension. And yes, paddlings were legal. The day went smoothly. We ate, we laughed, we scoped things out. The only blow? All the girls we grew up with had their eyes on the eighth-graders now. That stung.

We stuck close, walking home together if anyone had detention. Junior high was a different world— tougher, rawer, more about survival than education. The real troublemakers? Most of them were from the North End side of Goldsboro. Those boys were ruthless. They bullied, intimidated, and tested anyone new. I learned quickly to keep my guard up and my circle tight.

By then, I didn't trust male authority figures. I was quick to check any adult who stood too close or touched my shoulders. During P.E., a classmate patted me on the butt after a good shot. I snapped and slammed him to the ground. The coaches had to pull me off. "Don't touch me like that," I told them. I wasn't trying to fight—I just couldn't let my guard down.

Teenage years are awkward for everyone, but my trauma made mine more intense. Being a teenager is always an awkward time for any kid. You're caught in that strange space between childhood and adulthood where nothing quite fits right—not your clothes, not your emotions, and especially not your place in the world. For me, this normal teenage confusion was amplified by the trauma I carried from what happened when I was seven. My reactions were more intense, my boundaries more rigid, my need for safety more desperate than my peers could understand. I had to adapt quickly to the environment of junior high, not only to my changing body and mind, but also to the unwritten social rules that seemed to come naturally to everyone else. Fitting in wasn't just about popularity for me; it was about survival and safety. My crew gave me that security. We protected each other. Swapped clothes to stay fresh. Formed alliances when necessary. Rondo and I teamed up with Webtown boys like Big Red, Greg, and TJ. They had our backs.

We got tested by some eighth graders once and beat the brakes off them. From that moment on, we earned respect. I was finally moving into spaces few could.

But underneath it all, I still struggled. I couldn't absorb lessons like others, so they placed me in Special Ed again. It was humiliating. Kids teased me, called me slow. I wasn't having it—I fought back, literally.

Mrs. Julia, though, changed the game. She was patient, brilliant, and full of love. She told us how her father missed a chance to invest in McDonald's—and that life was full of choices. She treated us with dignity, even when other teachers didn't. Her belief in me reignited my desire to learn. She made all her students feel valued, yet we didn't have the courage to defend her, even though she always defended us. In that pivotal moment of my life, I realized my days of being afraid of other people's opinions were over. Embracing courage allowed me to fully absorb Mrs. Julia' s lessons. My hunger to learn grew, leading to more one-on-one time with her. Being seen as an outsider fueled my drive to become a better student and person.

One of my biggest advocates was Mrs. Warren. She was the 7th-graders' principal and really liked me. Anytime a teacher would send me or my friend Buddy to her office, she would give us lectures on how hard black people fought for us to be educated and we were doing a disservice to them by not learning. Mrs. Warren placed my desk in her office and made me do all my assignments and run errands for her. I didn't understand her philosophy, but I do now. She was protecting us from the consequences of not getting an education.

Mrs. Warren and her assistant, Mrs. Leslie, were good to us. Mrs. Leslie was cool. She spoke Ebonics and loved basketball. She never judged anybody, and her main goal was to understand the problems that children faced. I watched countless teachers give up on their students, but Mrs. Warren and Mrs. Leslie weren't like that. I thank God for them because I turned my grades around and passed the seventh grade with flying colors.

Seventh grade had been solid. My teachers believed in me, and I was growing into myself. But everything started to slip when eighth grade rolled around. It started with a broken heart.

Tanisha was my first love. Slim, light-skinned, and beautiful. We'd talk on the phone for hours. Just hearing her voice made my heart race. Her family was religious, and the teachers often judged our relationship. They called her the lady and me the tramp, but she chose me anyway. Eventually, she joined the girls' basketball team and left me for a boy on the boys' team. I was devastated—couldn't eat, couldn't sleep. School became a nightmare.

Months later, she came back around, but by then, I was seeing Brandy.

Brandy was a 7th-grade sweetheart—tall, dark, and beautiful. But I was still hurt and took it out on her. I accused her of things that weren't true. She cried constantly, begging me not to leave her. She'd walk miles just to see me, holding my hand like I was her whole world. I didn't deserve her.

At the same time, I started shoplifting with Buddy. When we first met he had an Afro, wore dress shoes with jeans, and wore a blue ski jacket all the time. He taught me how to walk into stores barefoot and come out with sneakers. We hit Belk's, Sears—anywhere that had what we wanted. One time, Buddy hid jeans in a tree with a hornet's nest. He came out swollen and screaming. He said it was a sign from God to stop. I didn't listen.

Eventually, I got too bold and tried to steal from a store with security cameras. Three women caught me so I shoved one and took off on my bike. That was the last time I stole. Buddy kept going—and ended up in reformatory school for a year.

With Buddy gone, and my heart still broken, I started failing eighth grade. Most of my friends moved on to high school. I was stuck. I spent the summer lying in bed, thinking about the embarrassment of repeating the grade. The same seventh graders I teased were now my classmates.

But that's when Brad entered junior high. Rondo's little brother. Chill, smart, and full of heart. When some eighth graders messed with him, he came to me. I handled it. From that day on, Brad rolled with me. He was my little brother, and I would defend him to the end.

Failure wasn't an option anymore. I got a job at Bob's Supermarket, five minutes from home. I stocked shelves and bagged groceries for $3.05 an hour. Working forty hours a week, I brought home $80 and gave most of it to my mom.

My new routine kept me grounded. Work, shower, watch Matlock and Murder She Wrote with Mom, then bed. I was focused. I passed the eighth grade. Rondo was more excited than I was. I ran through Green Acres yelling, "I'm going to high school!"

After years of chaos, I had finally found a rhythm. I wasn't just surviving—I was growing.

Chapter 4

FRESHMAN YEAR

It was 1986, and I was 15 years old when I entered my freshman year of high school. "Eric B. Is President" was the soundtrack of my soul as I stepped into that next chapter. I felt untouchable. My gear was on point, and just like that, the Green Acres crew was back together again. It felt like freedom—pure, unfiltered joy. I wasn't just moving on from junior high; I was stepping into a world I had only dreamed about. My freshman year at Goldsboro High School was nothing short of unbelievable.

The campus looked like a small college. Students from every walk of life filled the halls, dressed to impress, and the girls? Drop-dead gorgeous. Social status ruled everything, and fashion was your badge of identity. If your gear wasn't tight, you were labeled as lame. I wasn't having that. I doubled down at Bob's Supermarket, pushing Mr. Bob for more hours just to stay fresh.

One of the first things that stood out was the school's unique culture. There was a student fraternity called K-9-5, and they were the coolest cats on campus. They had step routines, secret handshakes, and their initiations were legendary. Their big brother was a guy named Super Davidson—a born promoter. If there was a big school dance, you could bet Super Davidson was the mastermind. His entrepreneurial grind was unmatched, and I watched from afar, inspired but hesitant. I considered joining K-9-5, but their initiation process wasn't for me. Plus, my loyalty was with my Green Acres brothers.

Goldsboro High was all about choices—and distractions. Off-campus lunch was an hour long, which for many meant mischief. Kids would get drunk, smoke weed, and hook up at home while their parents were at work. Some students even drove to school in their own cars. Fridays were sacred. After football games, Super Davidson would throw massive parties all over town. Being a Cougar meant something. Repping the blue and gold was a badge of pride, and rival schools hated us for it.

We were bold, loud, and always ready to scrap—especially when it came to other schools. Whether it was at the fair, on the court, or at the beach, fights were bound to happen. But through all the noise, we still had fun.

Back in the projects, my nights often ended at my cousin Tanya's house, watching Tyson fights and drinking Mad Dog 20/20 and Milwaukee's Best. Brad, Rondo, Omar, and I kept each other sane, laughing through the madness of our lives.

But freshman year flew by in a blur. I bought my first car, skipped over forty days of school, and eventually dropped out. Just like that, everything I had dreamed of began to crumble. My mom was devastated.

For the next two months I worked, and kept drinking Mad Dog 20/20 and Thunderbird. I couldn't believe that my dreams of obtaining a high school diploma were gone. Dropping out of school put me in a dark place. I was working full-time and living without purpose. Waking up every day and walking out of my mother's house was boring. During that dark time, I felt trapped in a cycle of self-loathing. My thoughts spiraled between anger at myself for giving up and hopelessness about my future prospects. Without a diploma, what opportunities would be left for me? The liquor helped quiet those thoughts, but it couldn't silence them completely. Work became just a mechanical routine—something to fill the hours and provide money for more alcohol. I moved through each day in a fog, present physically but emotionally detached from everything around me. The vibrant, ambitious part of me that had once dreamed of something better seemed to dim a little more each passing day.

I felt like I had proven everyone right—the teachers who thought I'd fail, the people who never expected a kid from the projects to make it. I was living up to their expectations. And it crushed me.

Then came my saving grace: a Greyhound ticket to Newburgh, New York, for my uncle's wedding. I packed my bag and headed north to stay with Aunt D.

Aunt D. was a light in my darkest season. She was my mom's older sister and a woman full of grace, wisdom, and encouragement. She didn't judge. Instead, she helped me find perspective and challenged me to see the lesson in the mess. She'd wake me up every day to job hunt, take me to Dunkin' Donuts—her favorite spot—and talk to me like I mattered. Her love was real.

Uncle Stick's wedding gave me a distraction and a role to play. We got fitted for tuxes, shopped for food, and prepped for the big day. That experience, small as it may seem, gave me a new sense of purpose. I was part of something again.

When I returned to North Carolina, I got my old job back at Bob's Supermarket and started grinding. I saved every penny, worked every shift, and got serious about turning my life around. Then, out of nowhere, a new opportunity opened: a chance to move to Brooklyn, New York.

And I took it without hesitation.

This was the next chapter. I wasn't sure what was waiting for me in Brooklyn, but I knew it had to be better than what I was leaving behind. And with that, my journey took a new turn—a chance to rewrite the script and chase a future I had almost lost.

Chapter 5

BROOKLYN RAISED ME

It was 1988, and I was 17 years old when I moved in with my Uncle W. in Bedford-Stuyvesant. It wasn't just a relocation—it was a rebirth. Brooklyn lit a fire in me. Everything felt electric. The streets were alive with the sound of boom boxes blasting Big Daddy Kane, the flash of gold rope chains swinging across chest-high top fades, and the confidence of men who carried the city on their shoulders. The women? Flawless. But if your pockets weren't deep, you didn't exist. The real stars of the block were the hustlers—cruising through the avenues in foreign whips with chrome rims, blaring bass, gold grills gleaming, and pagers lighting up like fireworks.

My mind was racing, hungry for it all. But Uncle W.? He slowed everything down. The moment I dropped my bag, he laid it out.

"Three rules," he said. "Get a job, go to school—or get out."

He didn't yell. He didn't threaten. He just meant every word.

Uncle W. was a man of order, and everything about him demanded respect. Feathered Stetson hats. Tailored suits. Shined Florsheim. He looked like he walked off the cover of a 70s jazz album. But it wasn't the clothes—it was his consistency. He taught me that real men take care of business and don't make excuses.

"If you mess up, fix it. Try harder. No one's coming to save you," he'd say.

I hit the streets running and landed a job at Kamco Supply in just six hours. Uncle W. was proud. He handed me some fresh work clothes, transit tokens, and lunch money. When I got that first check—$369—I felt rich. After giving him money for the bills and paying him back, I still had $200 in my pocket. For the first time, I felt like a man.

Then came Ronald—my childhood friend, my big brother by default. Ronald's family ran the back of

Green Acres and his roots were in Brooklyn, New York. He introduced me to 42nd Street, our kingdom on the weekends. We'd hit up the movies, grab pizza, snap photos under neon lights, then ride the A train to Brownsville and chill at his cousin Bethany's spot. That place was our safe haven—dominoes, dice, liquor, laughter. Ron was the ultimate player—short, stocky, smooth-talking. Every room he walked into, he left with a phone number—and often three women who didn't know about each other.

I was working. I was helping with bills. I carried groceries up three flights of stairs like it was nothing. I made sure my uncle never had to push his old grocery cart again. Uncle W. was more than a provider—he was my hero. I'll never forget when he hit the numbers for $15,000 and threw a party like he'd won twenty million dollars. Or that trip to Far Rockaway, fishing off the pier, buzzed off Budweisers, laughing until our sides hurt. We caught blowfish—nothing edible—so he bought fish from the store and played it off like we were pros.

Soon, I met his girlfriend, Betsy. She was cool, from a big family, and had just had his baby. She tried enrolling me in Boys and Girls High, but they turned me away—she wasn't my legal guardian. Their relationship was... complicated. Lots of passion. Lots of fights. One night it turned violent. I had to step in. I didn't like being in the middle of their mess, but I couldn't just stand by.

As life sped up, so did my curiosity with the streets. Crack was making teenagers rich. I asked around, and soon, I had thirty-three vials sitting in my uncle's apartment. I couldn't move it in New York, so I came up with a plan: FedEx. I shipped it to Big Red in North Carolina under a fake name. No signature. No trace. It worked. Every week, I hit that 10-minute-to-closing window at FedEx and sent off a new package.

Even Ron didn't know I was hustling. I stayed clean, stacked cash, and stayed fly—Adidas, Clarks, Nike, gold fronts. Then came Maryann—Bethany's daughter. We went on a double date, saw Batman with Michael Keaton and Jack Nicholson, grabbed pizza, and that was it. I fell hard. She became my everything... until she didn't. One day she told me it was over. No warning. I was crushed.

For three months, I ghosted Brownsville. I buried myself in work, school, and rhyming. Pain pushed me into productivity. I enrolled in technical school. Slept five hours a night and hit my grind. I worked toward rebuilding. Uncle W. and I barely crossed paths, but when we did, he checked in. He always dropped jewels and pushed me to stay focused.

Then I met Natasha. My God, Natasha. Smooth skin. Soulful brown eyes. Puerto Rican queen. Smart, silly, and down-to-earth. We connected instantly. She'd walk ten blocks through Bed-Stuy just to see me. It scared me—Brooklyn was wild. Shootouts, stickups, chaos. But she didn't care. She just wanted to be with me.

She held me down through everything—even when I got blackout drunk at school and she had to carry me home. She never complained. She just loved me.

But life started to unravel. My job paid less. School demanded more. My mom needed help, so I drained my savings to support her. Big Red sold off my stash. The hustle was done. I was broke again. Uncle W. sat me down: "What's going on?"

He wasn't mad—just disappointed. He fronted me money for school and job interviews. Natasha stood by me. Every morning, she'd come by the house and ride with me to school. But the distance grew. I started getting jealous. Possessive. Distrustful. And I ruined it. Natasha walked away.

Heartbroken. Lost. I dropped out. And that's when I did something stupid.

One Friday night, Malcolm—Ron's cousin—hyped me up to do a robbery. Ron begged me not to. I didn't listen and we got caught. The Guardian Angels, New York's citizen crime patrol, grabbed us. I was wearing the same clothes for three days in the holding cell. Everyone said I'd be released Monday.

They were wrong.

The judge looked me in the eyes... and sent me to Rikers Island.

And just like that, everything changed.

Chapter 6

RIKERS ISLAND

Damn, I messed up.

Rikers Island was the place that legendary rap artist Kool G Rap talked about in his song by the same name. Everyone on the bus was asleep or still trying to process the severity of their charges. When the bus finally made its way to C74, my body became numb. I instantly felt the switch flip inside me—that instant shift from vulnerable to vigilant. And in a second, all my fears went out the window.

As I entered the processing cage, I put on a straight face and placed my back against the wall. This switch, my survival mode, wasn't a conscious choice but an automatic response that had been hardwired into me since that day when I was seven years old. The switch shut down any part of me that could feel fear, replacing it with a cold, calculating focus. My senses sharpened, and I could feel the air currents as people moved around me, hear conversations from across the room, and spot potential threats before anything bad happened. This wasn't just survival; it was a complete rewiring of my nervous system. Years later, I'd come to understand that trauma had given me this gift—this curse—of being able to disconnect from my humanity when threatened. But in that moment on Rikers, I was just grateful the switch existed. Without it, I wouldn't have lasted a day.

After being processed, I was escorted to 4 Lower and was assigned a cell. Once my cell door was open, I lay down on my bed and looked out the window. Feeling sorry for myself wasn't going to help anything, so I fell asleep. I soon awoke to the sound of my door opening for breakfast. I was scared and hungry at the same time, but I had to man up. Everything that Kool G Rap said in his song was real because that initial walk to the chow hall turned into a full-blown fight with another dorm. Here I was fighting someone in the middle of a riot and watching some people get stomped out and wrestled to the ground. It was a crazy first day for me, but I was respected by my peers for engaging and standing tall for my dorm.

After breakfast, all you could hear was how everything went down and who the weaklings were in our dorm. The non-participants soon ran out of the dorm. After hanging out in the day room for an hour, I decided to head back to my cell and get some sleep. And once again, my cell door opened in preparation for lunch, which was at 12:15 pm. I headed to the dorm room and watched TV until our dorm was called to chow. This process happened for the next month during my stay at 4 Lower. Most of the guys I was housed with were locked up for armed robbery, murder, or distributing drugs. Some were already doing time in prison and were coming back to C74 to fight more cases. All I could think about was being released and never going back into the system again. Just making it to bed every night was a blessing because there was always tension in the air. Either someone was getting sliced across the face, stabbed, or beaten unmercifully for snitching. I rarely spent time outside to avoid the drama.

Everybody wanted to be tough and prove themselves worthy of being in our dorm. The guy who ran our dorm at the time was Christopher. Occasionally, new transfers would come in with more credibility and challenge the weakest person for their phone time or negotiate partial slots if they were associated in any way. But oftentimes, someone always got their head cracked for phone time. Christopher was from Jamaica, Queens, 6'2", weighed around 215lbs., with a distinctive round head. He always wore a black hoodie, Timberland boots, and a durag. Christopher would always spend his days plotting and figuring out ways to strong-arm his cellmates. He was known for taking people's commissary bags and then giving them out on credit for double the price. Deep down in my heart, I wanted to stand up for those individuals, but it wasn't my fight. I had to survive on my own and stick up for myself when the time came. The island was built on the "next man up" rule. Meaning that any dorm leader could be dethroned if he wasn't strong enough to defend his crown.

One day, this dude out of Brooklyn named Winston took Christopher's crown during a fight, and our dorm was never the same. Winston pressed people for everything, and if he didn't like you, chances were you got removed from our dorm. Winston had to be around 5'6" and around 235lbs. Never spoke much, but his presence was felt. For some reason, Winston didn't like me, so I eventually left the dorm, but I went out fighting. Unexpectedly, some of my cellmates jumped me, but I placed my back against the wall and punished them. I was too strong to be pushed around, and my arm reach gave me an advantage to strike their eyes and jaws. It didn't take long for those clowns to realize that I wasn't their average prey. Finally, one of the female correctional officers who observed the whole ordeal advised me to transfer to another dorm because I was going to get seriously hurt if I didn't. I stood in silence, so she made the decision for me. I was transferred to 4 Main, which had the reputation of being called the "House of Pain" because of the pain that was inflicted on people. Inmates were always leaving out of that dorm with severe stab wounds or their face slit from ear to chin. Once again, I was in an area of uncertainty and was confronted within ten minutes by some goons. One of the goons said his brother was in 4 Lower and sent word that I was a solid dude. They let me know I was protected, and no bodily harm came to me. I was so relieved about my current circumstances that I went to my cell and slept until the very next morning.

For the next three weeks, I stayed to myself and minded my business. Occasionally, I poked my head out to use the phone or watch TV, but for the most part, I stayed in my cell, hoping like hell that on my next court date, the judge would send me home. I loved 4 Main because it was more organized, and the inmates had total control of the dorms. If you disrespected a female officer, you were beaten down and run out of the dorm. Women were highly respected, and disrespect was never accepted when it came to them. They made sure that everyone got their six-minute phone call early in the morning to talk to their family or consult their attorney. The remaining slots were rated among the strongest in the dorm. After my brief stint in 4 Main, I was summoned to court to face my charges.

When inmates were taken to court, it was a completely different experience because inmates from all boroughs were gathered together in one area and placed in their respective holding cells. In this situation, most inmates positioned themselves at the front of the cell near the gate out of fear, while others stayed in the back of the cell. I chose to stay at the back and associate with the tougher inmates to avoid appearing weak and becoming a target. Those who stayed near the front gate often ended up being assaulted and victimized by other prisoners. You could tell when it was going down in other cells because you would hear the rumbling and inmates pleading for their lives. It would often start with the inmates yelling, "CO, CO, CO..." This tactic was used to get the attention of the corrections officer to remove them from their current situation and into a relief cell called the "why me?" pen. As an inmate on Rikers Island, you never wanted to go into the "why me?" pen because it labeled you as weak, and that tag followed you forever. I had my mind already conditioned to never go into that pen, despite what might have happened to me. I'd seen people get their sneakers, jackets, and jewelry taken in holding cells coming in and out of Rikers Island, but I still had my same Nike Air Max shoes and goose jacket that I arrived with. After all the violence of the morning, my name was finally called, and I was off to Brooklyn to be seen by a judge.

After arriving at court in Brooklyn, I met up with Malcolm, who was in terrible shape. He had a black eye, and his shoes, jacket, and hat had been taken. When it was our turn to stand before the judge, he decided it was in our best interest to release us on our own recognizance. We were happy with the decision. Our attorneys said they would be in contact for a plea agreement and our sentencing date. Hours later, Malcolm and I were released with huge smiles on our faces. We jumped on the train and went our separate ways. All I could think about was how I disappointed my uncle and what corrective action I was going to take to make this right. My uncle was happy to see me upon my arrival, but wanted to make sure I was okay mentally and physically. Those three months on Rikers Island felt like a lifetime, and things I didn't value, like freedom, privacy, food, and a basic hot shower, were valued.

After my release, Ron was at my house with a job, a start date, and a lecture for getting in trouble. I understood; I needed to do better. My new job was with an amazing company that did cleanup for oil spills that were created by major oil companies while transporting vessels through the oceans. Ron was my supervisor, so I came in with an advantage. Ron's crew was assigned the daily task of sweeping the beach's shorelines in Long Island. We would pick up dead birds and sea animals that were killed by the spill. And on other days, our team would spray off rocks on the ocean's shores with hot pressure washers. I loved my job because all our meals were free, and the pay was good! My very first paycheck was $700.00, and this was in 1990. I was working every day except Sunday with no time to enjoy the fruits of my hard labor. When I finally got time off, Ron and I went to downtown Brooklyn to shop and 42nd Street to hang out. I always looked up to Ron because he always had my back and included me in everything he did.

When Ron finally bought his first car from saving his money, it was a huge victory. Instead of riding the work van with fifteen people, we would pull up in his car. Life was good. After three months of saving money, I bought myself a 1978 Cadillac Coupe DeVille. It didn't sound like much, but everyone had Cadillacs in Brooklyn. I was working, driving, and fresh from head to toe. I bought myself a pager to act like I was important and started dating one of Betsy's Friends. Charlene was six years my senior, slim, and everything about her was bad. I first met her at a dinner hosted by my uncle shortly after I was released from Rikers Island. My uncle asked the two of us to walk to the store together to pick up some items for dinner. During this errand, we connected immediately—there was intense, meaningful eye contact between us. Later, when the dinner ended, I walked her outside to catch a cab. When we said goodbye, I gave her a kiss that made it very clear we would be seeing each other again soon.

Charlene possessed a smooth demeanor and exceptional street smarts. Her mental game was beyond what I could grasp at the time. She communicated her expectations very directly— she made it clear that to be with her, I needed to behave like a proper partner, as her beauty meant she could have chosen anyone. Every week, I gave Charlene money to get her hair, nails, and feet done. And she made sure the refrigerator was full with all the items I like to eat or drink. Going to visit her in Tompkins Projects in Brooklyn was dangerous because there were always thugs hanging out in her building, blocking the doorway and standing by the elevator. I expected the worst, but these dudes would always let me slide through.

Occasionally, Charlene and I would brave the freezing cold to walk to the Chinese restaurant together, and we genuinely enjoyed our time together. What made her unique was how she seemed to be guiding me, preparing me for future experiences I hadn't yet encountered. Our relationship was purely recreational since I couldn't sustain her lifestyle or match what she considered normal. Women of her caliber typically dated drug dealers who earned 100 times my entire paycheck in a single day. After two months of enjoying each other's company, Charlene revealed the tactics women use to manipulate men like me out of their money. She came to my uncle's house one Saturday specifically to warn me about being careful who I fall in love with, saying that "suckers are born every day." After delivering this advice, she gave me a long kiss and hug, thanking me for the time we'd spent together. I still respect her to this day because of her genuineness. Even though I was completely captivated by her and she showered me with love and affection, she recognized something in me that she didn't want to damage. Though I was hurt by the breakup, I understood the valuable lesson she taught me. Ron eventually told me it was a blessing in disguise, and it was best for me to move on. I did and kept my nose to the grindstone.

Ron knew I was good at rapping, so he hooked me up with this local producer to do a demo tape. We eventually went downtown Brooklyn to record a demo with this dude named Gam. He handled the sampling, production, and mixing of the track, which became very popular. People in our neighborhood frequently played it and asked when Gam and I would collaborate on another demo. I was all hyped up until things took a bad turn. Ron and I made the poor decision to hire someone to steal some car rims instead of purchasing them legitimately. Making matters worse, we allowed one of Ron's cousins, Jamie, to join and participate in the crime. We all got caught by the police. Because I was on probation, I was immediately shipped to the Brooklyn Navy Yard where they held inmates until their very first court date, while Ron and Jamie were released.

When I finally got released, my uncle gave me an earful along with my probation officer. Luckily, my probation officer gave me another chance by signing me up to this Vanguard Step Program in Brooklyn, and warned me that if another report came across his desk with my name on it, I would be shipped to prison for three years. I went back to the drawing board once again with the pressure of going to school, and I no longer had a good job to support myself. I was screwed. Gam and I still worked on music together and became good friends. We would always drink liquor and dream big, but looking at my current situation put me in a state of depression. I was wearing summer clothes in the winter and struggled to get by, until Gam came up with a scheme. He put Ron and me down on it, but I was hesitant because of my last conversation with my probation officer. I couldn't go to prison, let alone do three years, so I gracefully backed out. Gam said this was easy money because he had a tax refund check with someone else's name on it that came in the mail for $5,000.

My job would be to stick up the individuals who were going to use a fake identification to cash the check and take all the money. After sitting in class and evaluating my clothes, it was a no-brainer. I called Gam and agreed to do the job. Ron and I met in downtown Brooklyn. We had no weapons, even though Gam insisted that I take a handgun, but I declined. Getting caught in New York with a gun was like suicide, plus I was on probation. When the time finally came around, my mind was set on getting that money, but Ron wasn't. The guy that Gam told to cash the check did his job and met with Gam to split the take, and that's when I swooped in. Faking like I had a gun in my jacket, I said, "Don't make this a homicide, and nothing is moving but the money." The guy looked at me and hesitated for a second, but Gam suggested that he give up the money before they got shot. Gam could have won an Oscar that day because the guy never knew he was in on the plot. I grabbed the money and took off because robbing someone in broad daylight with people around was a sure ticket to prison. I ran for like six blocks before finding a cab stand to take me to Gam's sister's house.

An hour later, Gam showed up and we celebrated. All he talked about was how I rolled up with the killer face and robbed them with no gun. He gave me a split of the money, called a cab, and we went on a shopping spree. Ron rolled up and asked for a cut, but Gam said, "You don't get something for nothing in America," and we drove off.

From that day forward, Gam and I became good friends. He taught me how to dress and directed me on what name-brand clothes to wear. And when I went back to school, the women were all over me. I had a fresh cut every week, and I was sharp from head to toe. Gam was still cooking up schemes, and I was steadily declining them. One time, he came up with a plot to rob FedEx, one of the largest shipping companies in the world, because he had an inside contact who knew where their funds were located. I laughed at him and kept going to school. Then he got into carjacking, which was on a totally different level.

One time, he stole a 1990 Nissan Maxima that had premium features, including a sunroof and Bose sound system. The car was pearl white with a brown leather interior. During that period, our neighborhood had many cars that had been flipped because we had connections who could provide fake temporary tags with out-of-state license plates. At this time, Gam and I were involved in small-scale illegal activities, but we needed more consistent income because we were living an expensive lifestyle. We decided to head south to

North Carolina with eight ounces of marijuana. How crazy could we be to drive hundreds of miles in a stolen vehicle with fake tags and illegal substances in the car? I remember getting out of school one Friday, fueling up, and hitting I-95. I couldn't wait to pull up in the Maxima and look like a million bucks. I remember thinking that everything we had was fake. Gam's driver license, our car was stolen, and the plates were fake. To be honest, we didn't have the required inspection sticker, but we bought one from a mechanic friend in Goldsboro.

My mother and sisters were happy to see me because I showed up unannounced. My mother cooked me breakfast, and after I was done eating, I left to visit Rondo and Brad at their house. And once they saw that weed and smoked it, the word got out fast. Brad was out of it and had to go home. Omar was at work, but once his shift ended, we all hung out. They were happy that I was home and styling in the Maxima. Gam started tripping because Rondo didn't like him. I asked Rondo to ease up, but there was something about Gam that he didn't like. For the final two days, we sold weed, hung out, and chilled with multiple women, but that was short-lived. I needed to get back to school, and our weed was all sold out. Gam was fired up because of the money that was made in two days. He was letting our minor success turn him into Scarface, but I guess he never saw the end of the movie.

I was thinking more about graduating from Vanguard and possibly going to college. During my enrollment in their Step Program, I had the privilege of meeting some cool people. Adam, Alex, Kimmy, and Steve. Steve lived on Classon and Green Avenue, which was right around the corner from where I hung out. Steve and Adam were straight clowns, while Kimmy was humble and intelligent. Alex was very intelligent and came from a good family, but chose to do things because he wanted attention. Every day we would drive our program director Mr. H. up the wall. We were either showing up late or talking junk to our math teacher, Mr. B, who was drunk half the time. His favorite liquor was Absolute Vodka, and he made no secrets about it. Mr. B. and Ms. W. were our favorite teachers because they cared. They were into empowering the black youth with knowledge and field trips to the New York Stock Exchange and school rallies against budget cuts for educational programs. The Vanguard Step Program helped a lot of children in my position and was a staple in the Bedford-Stuyvesant community. They gave us a weekly allowance of $65.00 as an incentive to keep up our attendance. I struggled in school because Gam and I were making money in North Carolina.

Every other week, Gam and I would travel down, but that got overwhelming, so he stayed in Goldsboro while I purchased drugs and shipped them to him. I surrounded him with my homies to protect him, but Gam let the money go to his head. He isolated himself, and everything spiraled from there. Someone threw a brick in the back window of the Maxima. He was caught in the car with several ounces of weed, and the cops hauled him downtown.

Hours after that happened, I received an emergency page that included Gam's sister's phone number. I called her number, received the news about what had happened, and headed to Goldsboro. I hired an attorney for him but this situation put additional pressure on me. Fortunately, I was only weeks away from graduation, which would help get my probation officer to ease up on monitoring me. The roles in our operation had changed—I was now arranging for Gam's brother to purchase marijuana and ship it to me. However, I had to postpone this plan until after my graduation

Weeks before my graduation, Adam and I decided to dress alike and walk across the stage with our certificates of completion. I can remember how excited Steve, Alex, and Kimmy were. We celebrated afterward, and after having several shots of alcohol, I got into a cab and headed home. My uncle was excited that I was making an attempt at college, but little did he know I had failed my high school equivalent exam weeks prior to me graduating from the Vanguard Step Program. Despite my unrealistic optimism that I could succeed, my failure to prepare led to a harsh reality check.

Chapter 7

BACK TO NORTH CAROLINA

With Gam being in jail, I had to step up and travel to North Carolina. The commute was becoming exhausting. I became extremely cautious and vigilant because I knew that any mistake would result in a three-year jail sentence. After three months in jail , Gam was finally released, though the circumstances of his release were unusual. He didn't have any pending charges or a return court date, and he was in a rush to get back to Brooklyn. Things didn't add up, so I distanced myself from him. By breaking my ties with Gam and standing on my own, I decided to venture into something more lucrative, which would generate me over $1000 per day. That product was crack cocaine. I would buy weight from some of my Brooklyn friends who were in North Carolina and make a killing in Green Acres. I started with only $300, but my friends from Brooklyn would always give me more, which helped me tremendously. That one

$300 investment turned into $3000.00, and with my Brooklyn friends looking out for me on the next purchase, I was off to the races!

Green Acres was a hustler's dream because we could see everything coming in and out of our projects, and my friends and I never sold drugs to anyone we didn't know. When secret indictments were issued, most drug dealers would disappear from the scene, but my friends and I saw this as an opportunity. While others went into hiding, we would take advantage of the reduced competition on the streets. We'd celebrate our increased weekly profits by shopping at the mall and going to clubs. Whenever popular items like Air Jordans or the most fashionable clothing became available, I always had the means to purchase them. Rondo, Brad, Omar, and I hustled all day long. We were always tight and always moved together. If one person had, we all had. Even though there were other housing projects in Goldsboro, none of them could hold a light to Green Acres or our crew. People were scared to come to Green Acres because it was like entering a war zone. Shootings and even worse incidents were a regular part of life. I remember one friend of mine named Meek who would actively confront drug dealers who entered our neighborhood. He would literally beat them down in broad daylight, strip them of all their drugs, and distribute them to people among our clique. It was like watching Nino Brown 2.5, but happening right before our eyes in real time.

People in our area were buying drugs from him out of fear, but Rondo and I remained independent, which made him angry. This guy wasn't even from our housing projects and hadn't grown up in Goldsboro, yet he was controlling how things operated in our neighborhood—something that bothered both Rondo and me. One day, his ego got the best of him, and he confronted me about selling drugs in my project, and a fight broke out. He thought I would back down and be submissive like the other cowards, but I stood my ground.

After fighting for over a minute, my sister Gigi had to break us up. Following the altercation, we exchanged heated words, and I lost all respect for Meek from that day forward. Despite Meek being like an older brother to me growing up—he was five years my senior—our friendship deteriorated when he allowed his Nino Brown ego to come between us. The power had gone to his head, making him forget where he came from and who had been loyal to him all along. In fact, Meek was the one who threw a brick through the window of our Maxima out of jealousy months back when I was in Brooklyn. He couldn't stand seeing Gam and I making money selling weed in what he considered his territory, even though we never stepped on his toes or disrespected his operation.

When the smoke finally cleared and Rondo caught wind of what happened, there was a clear line drawn in the sand. Everyone in Green Acres knew not to mess with Rondo or his people. Rondo wasn't just talk—his reputation was built on action. He was a firecracker with a short fuse, and people gave him a lot of respect because he already had two cases in court for shooting others who crossed him. One time, he shot a person in the mouth with a .44 Magnum over a drug dispute, and I was right there to witness it. I remember how quick it happened—one minute they were arguing, the next minute Rondo pulled out that cannon and let it go without hesitation. Fortunately, the bullet passed through the person's jaw, and he survived, but it left everyone, including me, shaken. That incident showed me exactly who Rondo was when pushed to the edge.

I looked over at Rondo after the shooting like "what the hell was that about," but his nose was turned up with that crazy look on his face—the one that told you he was ready for whatever came next. It took some time for everything to register in my mind, but once reality kicked in, we got the hell out of Dodge. We moved fast, hiding the drugs and guns in our stash spots, trying to figure out our next move before the police swarmed the area.

Within ten minutes, the sirens were screaming through the projects. Amid the chaos, Rondo tapped me on the shoulder and said, "I'm wearing all of this. Don't worry about anything. When I get locked up, just bail me out." And that's exactly what happened. The next day, he turned himself in, got a high bond, and I hustled day and night to get the money to get him out. I was determined not to let my brother sit in jail a day longer than necessary. I even took a package from a dude who ran the North Side of Goldsboro — except I had no intentions of paying him back. This wasn't business; this was about loyalty. Rondo was my brother, and I was going to do whatever it took to get him free. I flipped that package quickly, turning the product into cash that went straight to Rondo's bail. When Rondo finally got out, I gave him what money I had left, and we were back at it again, hustling like nothing had interrupted our flow.

No matter what happened in life—good, bad, or ugly—Rondo was always there for me. That's what set him apart from others in the game. Most hustlers were only around when things were good, but Rondo stood firm when shit hit the fan. He never wavered, never questioned, never hesitated to put himself on the line. That kind of loyalty couldn't be bought; it was forged through years of having each other's backs when no one else would. There was no way I was going to let Rondo stay in jail under a $30,000 bond and not "rob Peter to pay Paul" to get him out. Meek might have thought he ran things, but we were about to show him who really controlled the projects.

Rondo and I started cutting our crack bigger, but at a lower price to steal money from all Meek's workers. Plus, we had that butter cocaine that all the crackheads loved because it was cooked with less baking soda and was potent. I also gave out crack on credit to individuals who lived in Green Acres. Once their welfare check came on the first of the month, I would make my rounds, collect my money, and sell more products. It wasn't long before his customers started drifting our way, first a trickle, then a flood. The economics were simple—users wanted the most bang for their buck, and we were giving it to them. The profits from crack were good, but it had a way of bending your soul and bringing out the worst in everyone.

Dealers were plagued with greed, and users with the empty hope of chasing that very first high. That was non-existent after their first experience with crack. As a dealer, you always saw things in real time because users' transformation did not happen in years; it happened in months. Women who were once beautiful became "rock stars." That was the terminology that dealers used because crack looked like little pieces of rocks and if you abused it, you became addicted to it. That white piece of rock was destroying people's lives and breaking up families. And I was the idiot who was at the forefront of all this madness.

There was something about seeing deprived children and women you once admired turn tricks for a high, but nothing took the place of me selling crack to a pregnant woman. That transaction still haunts me to this day because it was one of my younger friend's mother. She was in the wrong place at the wrong time, and I had to make a bad decision to prevent something worse from happening. My friend's mother was walking around my project at 3:00 am looking to buy crack. At the time, I was the only person around, so she begged me for a rock, and I declined. She begged me for crack for about an hour, and I finally broke down and sold her a piece. I didn't sell it to her for the money; I sold it to her to try and protect her from all the awful things that came along with hustling. I had seen women indulge in all kinds of crazy behaviors for the sake of crack. It was not unusual for individuals to extend their credit far beyond what they could pay, and when the first of the month came, they had zero dollars to their name after paying off their debt. There was no money left to put food in their children's bellies or clothes on their backs. Seeing children suffer killed my heart, so I would always give money back and walk the individual to the store to buy food for their children.

When Christmas came around, parents would steal and sell their children presents from under the tree. Crack had a way of getting the best of a lot of good people. I must admit that I wasn't a saint by any means because I was one of the biggest contributors to destroying families and communities that have left generational scars on people from around the world. Living in the moment when it comes to making money distorts your rational mind. I remember having nothing growing up, and now I had the best of everything. Instead of walking, my friends and I had rental cars for months at a time. The women we grew up with, who considered us bums in schools, were now in rotation with five other women for our attention. The Green Acres crew always dressed nice, rolled together, and had multiple women's houses we could go to at any given time. I never had any issue attracting women up with my game and looks. I could entertain the likes of multiple women at the same time. They would cook me food, iron my clothes, and keep my stash in their house. Occasionally, Maryann and I would mess around when I went back to Brooklyn to check in with my parole officer, but we never got serious again until I was hit with the unexpected news of her pregnancy..

I was excited but unprepared, so I started preparing for my unborn child. I would send boosters (aka shoplifters) out on missions to get baby clothes every day and pile them up in my mother's house. If crackheads were selling diapers or baby accessories I would buy them. Rondo, Omar, and I celebrated because they had sons, and my little man was on the way. Months had passed since the announcement of Maryann's pregnancy, and her due date was getting close. I had set everything up for my friends and me to drive to New York for the delivery, but I made the huge mistake of getting a rental with the wrong people, and it ruined my plans. The rental had to be returned, and I missed the birth of my son. I was pissed off at the world because I not only let Maryann down, but I let my son down as well! Out of frustration, I made one of the worst decisions in my life.

They say that trouble has a way of finding you when you least expect it, and it did. One night, two of my friends and I were hanging out outside a convenience store called Gold Wayne, which was located just outside of Green Acres. The night air was cold , and we were just passing time, talking about women and money—the usual hustler's conversation. Out of nowhere, five guys from another city rolled up into our neighborhood. They weren't from around there, and they carried themselves with an arrogance that didn't sit well in our territory. These outsiders had the wrong energy about them—too flashy, too loud, too disrespectful of the unwritten rules that governed our streets. We came up with a plan right there on the spot. The decision was made in seconds—we were going to rob them. It wasn't just about the money, though that was part of it. It was about respect and territory and showing these out-of-towners that they couldn't just stroll through our neighborhood like they owned it.

Even now, I feel guilty sharing this story because we robbed them at gunpoint, forcing a moment of terror that I can't take back. The weight of that night still sits heavy on my conscience all these years later. We robbed them at gunpoint, forced them to the back of the store, made them strip, and took everything they owned—wallets, jewelry, clothes, shoes, everything of value. There's a particular kind of shame that comes with knowing you've made another human being fear for their life. It's not something you can rationalize away, no matter how much you try to justify it with talk about the code of the streets or survival of the fittest. In those moments, I was a victim who became the creator of fear, the source of trauma for someone else. And that's a hard truth to sit with, even decades later.

As we ran across the field separating our projects, we decided to let off a couple of shots in the air to scare them even more. I could almost feel those out-of-towners' fear as they scrambled for safety, probably thinking we were firing at them instead of just trying to intimidate. I ran to my mother's house, and we started splitting up the money and jewelry. My mother's face changed the moment she saw what was happening. She pulled me to the side, her eyes filled with disappointment and concern, and asked me to leave because she didn't want any part of what just happened. There was no lecture, no yelling—just that look that mothers give when they know their child has crossed a line.

I left and went to my girlfriend's house, my mind still racing. I jumped in the shower and stood under the running water, thinking about how dumb that was. The hot water beat against my back as reality started to sink in. This wasn't just another hustle—this was armed robbery. The kind of crime that could put me away for years.

By the next day, all my friends knew Jerome, Monroe, and I had committed an armed robbery the previous night at the Gold Wayne convenience store. It was obvious who told them because Monroe was wearing some of the clothes of the victims we robbed. Jerome just rubbed his head and said, "We're going to jail because Monroe told everyone in the world about what happened last night."

Jerome was right because not even a week later, the detectives went by Monroe's house and charged him with five counts of armed robbery. Monroe hadn't just been picked up for questioning; they'd slapped him with all five counts, each one carrying forty years if convicted. That meant we all were facing two hundred years. Two hundred years. The number echoed in my head like a death sentence as I tried to process what it meant. My entire life could be spent behind bars for one stupid act.

Monroe would call me collect every day, pleading for me to get him out of jail, and I went into grind mode once again. I told Monroe to hold tight because it would be a minute since his bail was $50,000. One time, without paying attention, Monroe made a direct call and asked why I was still in Goldsboro. There was something off in his tone—something different, like he was hinting at something but couldn't place all the cards on the table. I told Jerome about the situation, and he didn't hesitate: "That nigger is snitching," he said, his face hardening before he instantly went into hiding. Jerome could read people better than anyone I knew, and if he said Monroe was talking, then Monroe was talking.

I kept hustling until I got a random phone call from my big brother Neil, stating that a detective was looking for me and he had four cop cars with him. Neil was one of my crazy homeboys. His switch was always on, and there were no limitations to what he would do to a person. One time, he stabbed a dude in the neck with a steak knife over a dispute. He had everyone in my town walking on pins and needles because if you had beef with him, there was hell to pay. He shot, stabbed, and robbed people randomly every day, but was a big-time dealer as well. One time, he pistol-whipped some off-duty officer in a club that he was a silent partner in, took their gun, badge, and truck, and ran it into a tree in our projects. After thirty minutes, all of us were joyriding in their vehicle. Neil finally shot holes in each one of the tires and broke all the windows. He was an unpredictable individual because he would flip out on some of his closest friends randomly.

His signature gun was a .45-automatic handgun. And he always had two of them with him. For some reason, Neil had a different kind of love for me because I would run up the minutes on his phone and try to impress women riding around with him, and he would just snatch the phone and give me an earful. I remember one time I went broke, and he put me back on my feet by blessing me with a bag full of crumbs that he got from a Kilo he just cut up. He told me to give him $250.00, and we were good. Let's just say I made a lot of money off those crumbs, and I was back in business. Monroe actually got hit in the head with a frying pan by Neil, and now I was facing the possibility of Monroe being a snitch.

Within minutes of receiving the call from Neil, a detective was at my girlfriend's door asking about me. I ran to her room and hid in the closet while he sat in her living room, trying to use scare tactics so she would snitch on me. The detective knew I was in her apartment but couldn't search the house without a warrant, so he left and gave her his business card. My girlfriend at the time tried to convince me that they had no evidence of me committing those armed robberies and that it would be wise for me to call that detective, which I did. After placing the call, meeting in a designated place, and getting sucked into a trap, I realized my girlfriend was wrong.

They handcuffed me and placed me in the back of the police car.

The detective put me in the interrogation room and started questioning me, but I followed street code: I stayed silent and requested an attorney. After three minutes of interrogation, they took me to jail. I couldn't believe that this was happening all over again, but this time I wasn't minor. The next day, I was placed in front of a judge and was given a $100,000 bond, but was assigned the best attorney in Goldsboro—J.D.

J.D. got people off murder charges, drug charges, child support—well, not child support—but he was good. I stayed in jail for a full month before he came to visit me because of his workload, but when he came, he had all the answers to my questions. My biggest question was why my bond couldn't be reduced. His response: "Monroe turned state's evidence against you, and here is your motion for discovery to verify it." Then he looked me in the eyes and said, "I am working on it, just hang tight," and walked away.

I was steaming and told Monroe what J.D. just told me through the gate because his cell was next to mine. Of course, Monroe denied it, but the paper didn't lie. I knew the worst was coming, so I lay on my bunk and gathered my thoughts. During a conversation with a childhood friend named Olie who knew Monroe, I wasn't surprised by what I heard. He laid out the facts, pointing out that I should have expected this since Monroe was known to be a crybaby as a kid. Given this and the fact that I was on probation, I knew my days were numbered. I couldn't imagine being sentenced to two hundred years in prison at nineteen years of age. My son wouldn't know me, and my mother probably would go to her grave with a broken heart. Many people in my life distanced themselves from me, and some faded away completely. While those days behind bars felt endless, there were moments of light. Throughout my time locked up, Brad never let me feel abandoned. When most friends faded away, he made the drive to visit, putting money on my books when he could. He'd show up on visiting days with updates from the streets, never letting me feel like I was missing everything. "Just hold on," he'd tell me. "We're waiting for you out here." Those simple words carried me through some of my darkest moments. Brad made sure I had what I needed; not just commissary money, but the knowledge that I still mattered to someone on the outside. When you're serving time, that connection to the world becomes your lifeline, a reminder that you haven't been erased from existence. Brad made sure I never forgot that. Every day, I would stare at the ceiling, wondering what would become of my life once my trial was over. I know J.D. was my attorney, but two hundred years was a long time if he couldn't win or get my sentence reduced. Luckily, Goldsboro was building a new jail and was housing inmates in an old storage warehouse until the completion of the new jail, which delayed people's time and slowed down the court proceeding process. For some reason, I was born with an innate ability to perform under stressful situations, and one night, I was lying on my bed, and I had an idea. It was crazy, but I knew it would work because we were locked up in an old warehouse. I know a lot of people thought about escaping, but the risk of fighting off guards and getting to the command center was too risky. Plus, I didn't want to get shot if the plan backfired, so I came up with a better plan.

I quickly realized that the temporary jail's design was flawed, and I took advantage of it. My dorm was situated on the far east side of the building, allowing me to hear the correctional officer approaching long before they reached our area. The challenge I faced was figuring out a way to escape quietly, ensuring I had an eight-hour head start before anyone noticed I was gone. I thought about this for a while before realizing that the upper trim of our walls consisted of old bricks, each two feet wide. This trim extended above the light fixtures, making it difficult for anyone to see into my dorm. Realizing I couldn't carry out this plan alone, I enlisted Olie to help. Olie thought it was a brilliant idea, but wondered how we would manage to chisel through the bricks without the right tools. Scaling the wall wouldn't be an issue because we could stand on the top of the shower wall and climb onto the rafter, but it was a waste of time without tools. My idea was temporarily thwarted, but I never got discouraged. My sole focus remained on getting the tools needed for our escape.

One day, I stumbled across some tools that were right in front of my face all along. Every day, I brushed my teeth and looked at the plumbing of the sink I most commonly used. I noticed that a hammer and chisel could be created with a little ingenuity. The elbow of the sink would be my hammer, and the long piece that the water flowed down in would be my chisel. I told Olie about my discovery, and we instantly pulled the sink apart. We also retained some advice from a brick mason who was in our dorm as well. He informed us that due to the age of the bricks, the mortar could be loosened with water once we removed several bricks from the structure. With this advice, Olie and I swung into action.

We called on some of our cellmates to beat tunes on the wall to cover the noise and alert us if any guards approached our dorm. Olie and I began our chiseling at 11 pm and continued until 2 am each night. This routine lasted for a week, during which we managed to break through several bricks, only to discover another layer of bricks behind them. I was confused, so we went back to the brick mason, who explained that having two layers of bricks was normal. However, once we got through the second layer, freedom awaited us. Olie and I became excited again, and then the unimaginable occurred. The second layer of bricks crumbled away, revealing the open highway and fresh air. Our cellmates were stunned, but Olie and I put on our jumpsuits, gathered our things, tied some sheets together, and descended the wall like Navy SEALS.

Chapter 8

THE ESCAPE

What am I doing?

That was my first thought as my feet hit the cold ground and I took off into the darkness at 2 a.m. that Saturday morning—seven others breaking out with me, hearts pounding like war drums.

I yanked off the bright orange jumpsuit marked "Wayne County Jail," stripped down to my boxers and a T-shirt, and ran. We hadn't thought past the breakout—no plan, no map, just desperation and instinct. The jail was on the north side of Goldsboro, ten miles from Green Acres. It might as well have been another country. But I didn't care. I was in survival mode, and nothing else mattered.

About three miles in, I hit familiar turf— neighborhoods where I knew people who moved weight at night. That's when I spotted Smalls. Just like fate, he was out hustling. I flagged him down, breathless, eyes wild. I told him everything in a rush. He didn't flinch and handed me the cash in his pocket and tossed me the keys to his "Rental Rock" (aka a car on trade from a crack head) without hesitation. Loyalty like that? You don't forget it.

I picked up the rest of the crew and dropped them off one by one. The city was wide awake with hustlers and street noise. As I cruised toward my mom's apartment, Brad appeared on the corner like divine timing.

"I just broke out. I need to disappear," I told him. He blinked, halfway thinking I was playing—until he saw Olie in boxers and a tee, jogging up the block behind me. Brad didn't say another word. He threw the door open and hit the gas.

We reached my mother's building, and I ran up, pounding on the door like a man on fire. When she opened it, her face dropped. She knew. I tried to lie and told her I had been bailed out. But my sister Sarah was there too, and she saw through it. I broke and told them the truth—that I had escaped jail, and I might never come back.

My mother didn't scream. She didn't cry. She gave me the kind of look only a mother can—quiet, deep, and filled with everything she couldn't say. I hugged her tight, grabbed what I could, and ran back to Brad's car, heart aching.

Brad had already made up his mind. "We can't bring too many people into this. We keep it tight. For you."

He took me to grab fresh clothes, then called Rondo and Omar—the only two he trusted to help. They came through and got me a room at the Best Western Hotel on the far edge of town. Olie wanted me to circle back for him, but my crew said no. It was too risky and this was about survival now.

They dropped me off with food, money, and a warning: stay low. I showered, lay on the bed, and stared at the ceiling, nerves rattling like loose change. I couldn't sleep. Every hallway footstep, every door creak—I thought it was the cops.

Finally, daylight slipped through the blinds. Check out was at 11:00. I waited, praying someone would show up. At the last minute, Brad pulled up.

"Get in the back and lay low," he said. "They're out heavy."

We picked up Omar and another homie named Jerry to take the wheel—neither Brad nor Omar had a license. He handed me a black hoodie and drove us out of the city limits to another hotel. I lay low there until Sunday night.

By then, we were front-page news. Seven escaped. Three had already been caught. Four of us were still breathing free air. My team had kept me safe and made plans for the next move.

That Sunday night, we packed into the car and drove to Richmond, Virginia. I was catching a bus to New York. The ride was quiet, filled with forced laughter and heavy hearts. We all knew the truth— this might be goodbye.

At the terminal, I hugged each of them tightly. They slipped me some money—$300 in my pocket, a black hoodie on my back, and a one-way ticket in hand. I boarded the bus at 1 a.m. and my heart was pounding. Every minute, I expected them to rush me. But they didn't.

I rode in silence and slouched in the back. My nerves were shot. I couldn't go to my uncle's—the police would be there and couldn't go to my ex's— we'd been done. My only shot was Joyce Ann's house—Maryann's mother.

Joyce Ann opened the door like she'd been expecting me. No questions. Just a place to breathe. I gave her half my cash. Maryann didn't even know I was there—or that I had broken out.

I thought maybe we could fix things. But Maryann had moved on, and I couldn't blame her.

The hustle warps you and makes you selfishly forget what matters until it's too late.

Now I had nothing. Just three outfits, no plan, and a hoodie in the dead of winter.

Still, Joyce Ann let me stay. Karen came back into my life, too. Ron—solid as ever—was working in waste management. He let me run his routes using a fake name. I rode the back of a trash truck at night and made $300 a week. I watched my son in the morning and hung out with Karen on weekends.

Eventually, I moved in with Ms. Connie, Maryann's aunt. I told her the truth: I was a fugitive. She just laughed. "Why should I believe that?"

But she fed me, housed me, and kept it real. I chipped in when I could. Karen and I had fun. We grilled all the time , watched Def Comedy Jam, and argued Bulls vs. Knicks. I was all Jordan, all day.

Things felt normal—for a moment.

Then it all crashed.

Somebody close betrayed me. Word got out. Ron warned me that the cops were sniffing. I told Karen everything. She listened, calm. Then she made a call to her mother in Phoenix and immediately got me a flight.

My alias was Donnell Shields. The fake ID would get me there.

That night was tense. I stared out the window, half-expecting a knock. But nothing came.

At the airport, I breezed through. My heart was in my throat the whole way, but no one stopped me.

I was free—for now.

Chapter 9

WELCOME TO PHOENIX

As the plane touched down in Phoenix, I exhaled, finally letting go of the tension I had been carrying for what felt like years. The desert air felt different—lighter, drier, but full of uncertainty. Nobody knew where I was except Karen and her mother. I had vanished from the world, living as a ghost, a fugitive from justice, hiding in plain sight.

Karen's mother was the first to greet me at the airport. She hugged me tight, not saying much, just holding on as if she understood the weight I carried. She was a strong, grounded woman, and something about her presence made me feel safe. On the drive to her home, she didn't pry or press for details. She just drove in silence, occasionally glancing over at me with eyes that held more empathy than words ever could.

During that quiet ride, my thoughts raced. I thought about my son—his little face, his laugh—and all the bad decisions that had led me to this moment. I was facing two hundred years behind bars, an escape charge, and the betrayal of someone I once called my brother. Monroe had sold me out for a lighter sentence, and the pain of that betrayal still burned hot in my chest. My emotions were a whirlwind—anger, fear, sadness, and a quiet resolve not to break.

When we finally pulled up to Karen's mother's house, I stepped inside and exhaled again—this time from sheer relief. I took a long, hot shower, devoured some McDonald's, and collapsed into bed, finally feeling some sense of peace. But peace doesn't last long when you're on the run.

The very next morning, I was up early, hitting the streets looking for work. I knew I couldn't just sit around. I had to stay busy. I ended up landing two jobs—one at a car wash during the day and the other at Burger King in the afternoon. It wasn't glamorous, but it was honest. Within two weeks, I was helping with the bills and feeding myself. That alone gave me a sense of pride I hadn't felt in a while.

Karen and I talked on the phone every day, exchanging "I miss you" like teenagers. It didn't take long before she packed up her life and moved out to Arizona with her children. Her mother welcomed them into her home with open arms. The house felt full again—laughter, energy, and life. Her mother became a steady figure in all our lives. She cooked, she watched the kids when we needed space, and she never judged my past. She became my second mother, one of the few people I trusted completely.

The work grind was constant. Scrubbing cars and flipping burgers might not sound like much, but it was my anchor. It kept my mind off everything I was running from. Still, the fear never left me. Watching America's Most Wanted each week felt like playing Russian roulette with my conscience. My picture could pop up at any moment.

Karen knew I was struggling with the weight of it all. She and her mom kept me distracted. We'd take the kids to the park, shoot hoops, and go to the movies. Being around those children helped fill the hole left by being away from my own son. Their joy became my comfort. Their laughter drowned out my anxiety.

Six months passed. My relationship with Karen was strong, and I was finally beginning to breathe. The carwash was good, but not enough. I wanted more. One of the guys at work mentioned a temp agency hiring for a company that made airbags. I jumped at the opportunity.

After submitting my application and passing the drug test, I got the call—I was hired. Karen and I were ecstatic. The new job came with better pay, which meant we could finally get our own apartment. The very next day, I gave notice to both Burger King and the carwash. I thanked them for the opportunity, knowing they were part of what had kept me afloat.

But things changed quickly. Karen was proud of my new job, but she hated that it came with new surroundings, especially some of my coworkers. The long hours turned into an issue as well. Every day I came home, I had to explain myself and answer questions.

Our relationship, once light and loving, became heavy and combative. Arguments erupted over the smallest things. My only place of peace became work, and that only lasted until the shift ended.

By the time Karen was six months pregnant with our child, our home felt like a battleground. Then came the breaking point. One night during a heated argument, Karen asked me to leave.

I respected her request and packed my things. When I got outside, there were police everywhere with their flashlights and guns drawn. They were shouting commands. I was handcuffed immediately and taken to Madison Street Jail in downtown Phoenix.

The booking process felt surreal. Fingerprints. Mugshots. Chains. All I could think about was North Carolina—and the storm waiting for me back there. Within three days, a U.S. Marshal showed up to escort me back.

Karen and her mother both came to visit me before I left. Karen cried. Her mother held her close but kept her eyes on me. I could feel the disappointment and the heartbreak in both of them.

When the Marshal arrived, he chained me to his wrist and made sure I saw the firearm holstered on his hip. "Don't try anything," his eyes said.

We were the first ones on the plane out of Phoenix—and the first ones off when we landed in North Carolina.

Reality had come back to collect its debt.

Chapter 10

WAYNE COUNTY JAIL

I was back in Goldsboro.

It was 8 p.m., and the jail was buzzing with tension. Most of the inmates were awake, pacing, gambling, laughing too hard at things that weren't funny — just trying to survive another night behind concrete and steel. Once I was processed and placed in a holding cell, the word spread fast that I had been caught. It felt like the whole jail already knew before I even got my jumpsuit on.

Then something unexpected happened — something that almost felt like divine intervention. The jailer placed me in a pod with some of my childhood friends… and my cousin Percy.

Percy lit up like a kid on Christmas. "Yo!" he said, laughing as he looked me up and down. "How the hell did you end up in Arizona?"

We both laughed. That kind of laugh that's layered with pain, pride, and disbelief. He was genuinely hyped to see me, not because I got caught, but because I had embarrassed the Goldsboro judicial system. I'd made it out and stayed on the run for 3 years. In his eyes, I was a hood legend, a living myth walking back into the system in cuffs but with my head still high.

But me? I just wanted to know about my family.

I hadn't seen them in years. I asked about my mom.

Percy's face shifted. "Your mom's? She moved to New York."

I stared at him. "Are you serious?"

He nodded. It was real. Everything had changed. While I was gone, the world kept spinning. My mother had moved. My family had scattered. That realization stung deep, like I was coming back to a world I didn't even belong to anymore.

We sat and talked for hours, just chopping it up like we were back on the porch. It brought a strange comfort. I hadn't laughed that much in years. But eventually, the exhaustion hit. I showered, lay down on that stiff jail mattress, and tried to sleep. My body rested, but my spirit stayed restless.

The next morning came fast.

I was pulled from my cell and taken to court to face the music. I had already prepared myself for the worst: new charges, an escape charge, maybe even a judge ready to throw the book at me.

But when I stepped into the courthouse holding room, **there he was — J.D.**

He was still my attorney - still riding with me.

He hadn't walked away when I fled. He hadn't dropped my case when I crossed state lines and disappeared into the Arizona heat. Instead, he stood up. He showed up.

He walked into that room, tapped me on the shoulder with a thick manila folder, and gave me a half-smile like only he could. "I told you I was gonna take care of this case," he said, chuckling. "But you ran out on me."

That laugh—man, it lifted a weight I didn't even realize I was carrying. Because for the first time since getting caught, I didn't feel alone.

J.D. wasn't just any lawyer. In Goldsboro, his name rang a bell. Folks called him "Rapping' J.D." because of the way he flowed in the courtroom. He had that rhythm, that presence. He didn't just defend his clients—he painted pictures, told stories, and turned the courtroom into a stage. He took all the high-profile cases, especially the ones the streets respected. If you were a known hustler or caught up in a major indictment, chances are you wanted J.D. on your side.

And now, he was on mine. Again.

He looked me in the eye and said, "Keep your head down. Let me figure this out. You're gonna be okay."

Considering I was now facing five counts of armed robbery and an escape charge, I held onto his words like oxygen. He made me believe I had a shot, even when everything else told me I was done.

Later that day, I was shipped off to Central Prison to await sentencing.

The bus ride felt like it took forever, even though the prison was only an hour away. Central was the place I'd heard about since I was a kid. They said it was hell on earth. Inmates were stabbed to death in their sleep. Men violated, broken, turned into ghosts behind those walls. They didn't call it "The Wall" for nothing. Once those gates were locked behind you, all you saw was concrete and time.

But I had already survived Rikers Island. I knew how to flip that switch.

That switch inside me—the one built from trauma, from the moment I was violated as a boy and learned that no one was going to protect me— flipped the minute I stepped off that bus. I became someone else. My eyes sharpened. My back straightened. I was ready for whatever.

Processing was humiliating. Strip naked. Bend over. Spread your cheeks. Cough.

After that, I was issued my DOC clothes and taken to my dorm.

My dorm was in chaos. Cards slapping tables. Fights are breaking out. Guys flexing for power. This wasn't jail—it was the jungle. But I moved quietly. Observed everything. J.D. had told me to keep my head down, and I followed his advice like it was scripture.

I connected with a dude named Ryan from Charlotte. He was funny and reckless—but real. He had a murder case and a blade in his waistband. He slept with his boots on and didn't trust anybody. He was the only man I'd seen check Gabe—the dude running the dorm—right in front of everybody.

One day, this white kid named Scotty, who was being extorted and "protected" by Gabe, got slick with Ryan. Ryan barked, "I'll slap the taste out of your mouth and wait for your boss to do something."

Gabe didn't move.

That was the day his rule ended. When he got transferred, Scotty was jumped, robbed, and humiliated. The same inmates who pretended to protect him turned on him in a heartbeat. He walked around with a black eye, a broken spirit, and no voice. I stayed clear. Rikers taught me—stand on your own or get stomped trying to lean on others.

Eventually, I got transferred to Hoke Correctional Facility. It was a blessing.

I finally had my own room and was able to visit the yard three times a day. There were even Friday night movie rentals from Blockbuster. I went from a war zone to something resembling peace. But I was still caged. Still facing 200 years.

I kept reading, learning, and preparing. Guys told me I'd probably get a break since it was my first adult charge, but that didn't ease the pressure. That time still hung over me like a noose.

Two months later, I got a letter from J.D.. My court date was set. December 16, 1993. Back to Wayne County.

The night before my sentencing? A blur. I can't remember anything. Maybe I slept. Maybe I didn't.

I just remember the next morning—shackled, in a van, praying the entire ride.

When I arrived at the courthouse, they put me in a private room. A few minutes later, J.D. walked in and sat across from me with a manila folder. He said, "Lawyer, Judge Russell Duke is on the bench today. He's tough. But I think we can make this work."

He opened the folder and slid the plea across the table.

"I got four of the five armed robbery charges dropped. You plead to one. Fourteen years. Seven are mandatory. But you work, you earn, you gain time—you'll get out earlier. Escape charge? Gone. Thrown out."

I couldn't believe it.

From 200 years… down to maybe 7?

When I entered that courtroom, I sat beside J.D. He tapped my hand and I stood tall. Then he went to work like a man on fire. He told the judge my story—where I came from, what I'd been through.

I wasn't a criminal, but a product of my environment and that I still had value.

He said, "Your honor, if the court gives up on this young man now, then the justice system has failed him. There is more life to live. Redemption is still possible."

The courtroom fell silent.

The judge looked at the DA. "You good with this?"

"Yes, your honor."

The judge signed it. It was done.

I was escorted to the back to speak with J.D. one final time. We shook hands. He told me he was proud of me and told me to stay focused.

As I was led away, an old white bailiff—one who had watched everything—stopped me. He looked me dead in my eyes and said, "Lawyer, you're a good kid. I want you to go in there and make something of yourself. And I don't ever want to see you back in this courtroom again. You understand?"

I nodded. "Yes, sir. I promise."

We shook hands.

That was the last time I saw him.

But his words stuck. Something about the way he said it. The sincerity in his voice. It hit differently.

That day marked the beginning of something new.

I still had time to do—but for the first time, I believed I could come out of it better than I went in.

Chapter 11

HARNETT COUNTY

The days of worrying about my time were now over. The only thing I could control was what was ahead of me. The switch that protected me on Rikers and during my escape now needed to adapt to a different challenge: endurance. Prison wasn't about surviving a moment of danger; it was about surviving years of confinement without losing myself.

Lawyer Johnson didn't exist anymore because once I was in the custody of the Department of Corrections, my name changed into a number. My new identity was 01203-NY. I entered the gates of Harnett County in January of 1994 with no idea of what to expect. I was entering a facility with 1,000 inmates. And Harnett County was massive compared to most correctional institutions. It was inmate-driven, and there were rules in place that could cost your life if you violated them.

Most people fall victim to the devices that prison has to offer within months because they can't hide their true identity. If someone's sexual preference was being with the same gender, then prison had a way of pulling that out of them. I respected people who embraced themselves versus the ones who tried pretending they were someone they weren't. It was common practice for inmates to wait at the intake building to scoop out their future partners in hopes of swaying them over with perks that would come in the form of money, canteen, or drugs. Once these inmates chose each other, it was written in stone that their partner was off limits. Violating someone's partner by flirting or trying to engage in any physical activities was a recipe for death in prison. There were also loan sharks who lent inmates money for fifty cents on every dollar they borrowed. And if you didn't have their money when it was time to collect, you would get a visit from their henchmen, giving you a verbal warning that you must pay interest on your late payment, and everything must be paid in full on the following Friday or things would be handled in a different manner.

Harnett even had bookies who took bets for every major sporting event. Everyone was hustling. People were hustling fried chicken, cigarettes, and everything you could think of. There were even people renting out Hustler and Playboy magazines per night. I loved Harnett because it was an awesome learning experience for me, plus I was a part of a solid dorm. Dorm C-1 housed my mentors, who were mentally prepared to return to the streets. I was blessed to be around a handful of men who made my transition into the prison population smooth. Sam was one of those men. He was from Raleigh, North Carolina, and was a stand-up dude. He was locked up for killing someone during a fight and was sentenced to forty years.

Sam was a loan shark who loved playing basketball and betting on sports. He was short with a long beard and always hung out with his friend Tucker, who was serving a life sentence. Sam was already twelve years into his sentence prior to us meeting, and I was coming in as a rookie with three months under my belt . Sam was the big brother who kept me away from a lot of bad things that were going on. I believe God puts people in our lives to learn something from, and Sam was one of those guys. Always humble and never flustered when a problem occurs. Then there was Charles, who was from Greensboro. He was a very funny dude, but would stab you in a heartbeat.

I called him the nighthawk because he enjoyed catching inmates who were adamant about their sexuality as men until the lights went out and all that went down the drain. I would laugh because he exposed hardcore inmates as frauds. Charles was good at reading people and got a kick out of watching people fold under pressure. He would always say never fake who you are because, at the end of the day, you are who you are. Sam and Charles were my big brothers, but Ken was my brother in faith. Ken was in jail for having a shoot-out with some cops during an armed robbery that went bad. From my understanding, he watched one of his friends get killed in the standoff. Oftentimes, he would have nightmares about that situation and wake up screaming in the middle of the night.

I noticed that everyone was dealing with their mental issues, including me. Most people couldn't deal with being confined and fighting their demons, so they were spared by taking high dosages of medication. Some people suppressed their issues by lifting weights, playing basketball, or enrolling in trade schools or college. That is what Ken and I did. He enrolled in college, and I went to school to obtain my GED. There were times when he tutored me and answered all my questions when I was preparing to take my GED exam. Things that were hard for me were water under the bridge for him. Even though Ken was a genius, he was also a live wire—always ready to fight or kill somebody.

Once he was trying to fight Sam, but Sam just laughed and walked away, only because he didn't want to pull me into it. This guy would walk around in the yard with a blade in his shoe, waiting for the opportunity to shank someone. Ken was the one who introduced me to Islam and was there when I took my declaration of faith. And gave me books to build my foundation in Islam. Then I met Darius. He was from Coney Island and was locked up for murder. Darius was on a different level from anyone in our Islamic community. He was disciplined, didn't eat meat unless it was halal, and lowered his gaze in the presence of all women. Sam thought he was crazy because he ate with his hands and wouldn't take a shower in the presence of another man. He actually loved being in the hole because it brought him closer to God through meditation and prayer. When he finally got out, I would expound on the things I had learned and absorb any new lessons he was willing to share.

We walked to breakfast every morning and to dinner every night, going over the books that he tasked me to study. The majority of his books came from Iran. Their Islamic Center would send them to him upon request. Being mentored by Darius and comprehending all my reading material made me realize that I never had a learning disability. All this time, my willingness to learn came from laziness. This realization was both liberating and sobering. How much of my life had I wasted believing I wasn't smart enough? How many opportunities had I missed because I'd accepted others' assessments of my limitations? These questions fueled a hunger for education that extended beyond religious studies. I threw myself into studying for my GED and Electrical Wiring Certification, focusing on these goals with a focus and determination I'd previously reserved only for hustling. And I did it all within eight months. That moment in my life lit a fire in me.

I enjoyed being knowledgeable and disciplined in my prayers and freeing my mind from all the B.S. that was going on at Harnett. For a minute, I thought being in love and behind bars would work, but it turned out to be a disappointment. My heart was broken, but I had to stay strong. I developed rituals to keep my emotions under control. Cold showers became a way to shock my system back to the present when memories threatened to overwhelm me. Meditation—a practice I learned from Islamic teachings but adapted to my needs— helped me observe my thoughts without being controlled by them. Prayer five times daily created structure and connection when I felt most alone. That was the only way I could stay focused. Others in my situation lost it and let their emotions bleed out into fights. I even had dorm mates who would smack their spouses or girlfriends on visits because they weren't home at a certain time to answer their phone calls. I thought that was selfish. How could you expect a woman to put her life on hold during your incarnation?

Every inmate had their own way of dealing with their emotions because disappointment arrived in the mail every day. I admired the OG's approach because their philosophy was different. They wouldn't allow their thoughts to be consumed by things they couldn't control in the outside world, so these men encouraged their girlfriends and spouses to have fun while they were locked up. But once they were released from prison, everything went back to normal. They were masters at controlling a woman's mind and not her body. Those words of wisdom put me on a different path, so I didn't have time to hurt. I focused on taking advantage of every opportunity that the correctional institution had to offer. When everyone was sleeping, I would always read my Quran or books that enlightened me to become a better person. I shut my emotions down from the outside world and cared less about receiving letters. I focused on doing my time and not letting my time do me. Prison has a way of making you find yourself and come to grips with reality. In the real world, you could run away from your problems, but when you're confined, there is no more running away. I had been running from my demons for seventeen years, and now I had to confront them.

My self-healing always came from being defiant, fearless, and pushing the envelope without regard for consequences. Most people would absorb their pain through alcohol and drugs, but mine was through crime. I never understood why I was such a disruptive kid in school, and why being suspended for ten days for acting out never bothered me.

I spent countless nights in my dorm staring at the ceiling, trying to make sense of the trajectory my life had taken. How had I gone from a happy child with simple dreams to someone capable of armed robbery? What had changed inside me?

During one particularly long night of reflection, as I lay on my prison bunk reviewing my life choices,

I began to notice patterns. The constant anger. The mistrust of authority figures. The way I'd throw myself into dangerous situations without concern for consequences. The emotional walls I'd built that even those closest to me couldn't scale.

Then it dawned on me, and the picture became clear. All my problems began when I was molested as a child by my next-door neighbor.

This revelation hit me with the force of a physical blow. The memory I'd buried for so long—I had tried to outrun through crime, through hustling, through constant motion—was the root of everything. That single violation had fundamentally altered how I saw the world and my place in it. It wasn't just something that had happened to me; it had become the invisible lens through which I experienced everything else.

I realized that after the abuse, I started viewing vulnerability as weakness. I learned that trust led to pain. I had come to believe that no one could protect me but myself. These weren't conscious lessons—they were survival adaptations that my seven-year-old self had made, and I'd been living by their logic ever since.

The switch I had developed—that ability to shut down emotion and operate on pure survival instinct—hadn't formed by accident. It had been born in that basement, my child's mind desperately creating a mechanism to endure what was happening and to ensure it never happened again.

And that's exactly what happened to me. After connecting my childhood trauma to my self-destructive path, something shifted inside me. I wasn't just serving time anymore; I was using time to serve my own healing.

One Sunday morning, I was lying on my bed when the dorm officer yelled out that I had a visitor. The words hit me like a wave. Visits weren't common, especially unannounced ones. I threw on my prison best and walked to the visitation room, my heart pounding with a strange mixture of anxiety and hope.

When I stepped into the room, there they were— my mother, Omar, and my big sister Gigi. It had been four long years since I'd seen any of them. My eyes scanned the table full of snacks they had brought, but I couldn't touch any of them. It was Ramadan, and I was fasting. Even so, my spirit was full. We sat down, laughing, catching up, and cracking jokes. Gigi and Omar did most of the talking, and I hung on every word. But my mother... she barely said anything.

She kept her head down and avoided eye contact. It didn't take much to sense her fear, her heartbreak. She had every right to worry—I was still her baby. And this place, this environment, this life—it wasn't supposed to be mine.

After a while, I asked Gigi and Omar to step out so I could talk to Mom alone. I needed that. She needed that. I held her hands and told her I was okay and that I was becoming better. That I was going to come out of this not as a victim, but as a man. We laughed about my escape and the time I spent on the run, the kind of laugh you let out to keep from crying. And then the visit ended.

I hugged her tightly, kissed her cheek, and made a silent promise to do better.

That night, I cried. Quietly, into my pillow, the same way I had as a little boy. I prayed harder than I ever had before. I begged God for forgiveness—for the pain I'd caused my mother, for the lives I'd disrupted—and I asked for a transfer. A new environment. A chance at peace.

By Thursday, my prayer was answered. I was being transported to Tillery Correctional Facility—a minimum-security prison tucked away in the middle of farmland, known for its strict probationary structure. If you were considered an escape risk, this was where they sent you to prove yourself.

The moment I arrived at Tillery, I was introduced to Lieutenant G., the man behind the infamous "inmate or convict" speech. He drilled it into everyone that you either adapted to the system or the system would crush you. After that, I was processed, assigned to a dorm, given my work detail, and told the name of my case manager.

My first goal was clear: find the Imam. Every prison Islamic community had a leader, and I needed to connect with mine. His name was Brother Henry.

Brother Henry had a calm intensity about him. Always clean-cut, boots shined, clothes neatly pressed. The staff respected him. The inmates respected him. And slowly, I began to as well.

We would walk the yard together, often while he ate butter pecan ice cream, talking about faith, structure, and discipline. He was tough on the brothers in the community, but it came from a place of love and expectation. He didn't let the system take his identity, and I admired that.

Classes were held three times a week. Jumah every Friday. There was also an assistant Imam—Brother Scott. He was tall, humble, and sharp. Scott would wake me up for Fajr prayer every morning, then we would go to breakfast and talk about Islam. He and I shared a love for history, and it bonded us.

Eventually, I was assigned to Scott's section—metal shop. The job was simple: build bunk bed frames and lockers for prisons across North Carolina. Our supervisor, Mr. H., cursed like a sailor but was fair and well-liked. He gave us space to be men, but cracked the whip when it was time to work.

At first, I was just a laborer, organizing and stacking finished products. It was grueling, hot, sweaty work in a building with no AC, surrounded by the stink of nearby hogs and dairy farms. The heat was unbearable, the air thick with humidity. And if the stench didn't break you, the snakes would. Still, I loved it. It gave me purpose.

Tillery had its system. A six-month probationary period with the chance to transfer to a level one medium-grade facility if you don't get into trouble. Many failed. Some escaped and got caught hours later, wandering in cornfields. I wasn't about to make that mistake again. My mother's tears were still etched in my mind. I stayed focused, stayed sharp, and completed my six months.

From there, I was transferred to Neuse Correctional Facility in Goldsboro, North Carolina.

It felt like a homecoming.

Omar drove my mom and Gigi to see me regularly. His loyalty was unmatched. The Islamic community at Neuse was strong, organized, and respected. At the center of it all was Kendric.

Kendric had the unit on lock. If anything went wrong—chaplain overstepping, Ramadan meals delayed—Kendric handled it. He knew the Department of Corrections' policies better than the officers. He had access to every dorm. And when new Muslims arrived, he was the first to greet them.

If they needed hygiene products, food, or prayer rugs, the Islamic community provided it. We had a donation fund collected every Friday to support our community . Kendric was all muscle, bald, 235 pounds, and built like a linebacker. But more than that, he was deeply respected.

Eventually, I became his assistant Imam. It wasn't a position I sought—it came with weight. But Kendric saw something in me. I led Wednesday night classes, taught new brothers, and represented the community. Mr. R., the head of Neuse, supported everything we were doing. When the chaplain tried to cancel our Jumah, Kendric went to Mr. R. and had it reversed that same day.

Kendric was a leader, but also a brother. I learned more from him than I could put into words.

Then came the test.

One day, I walked into my dorm to find a white inmate beaten half to death. Blood was everywhere. No one would talk. I knew who did it, and I knew why. It was Black History Month, and racial tensions were high. But this wasn't justice— it was brutality.

I couldn't stay silent.

I told the men they were cowards. I told them to jump me like they did him. Someone shouted, "Why do you care about that cracker, Lawyer?"

I stormed out and found Kendric—he was in the shower. I yelled, "Strap up! It's wartime."

He jumped out, still soapy, trying to calm me down. "Brother, you can't do this. You're not just a man anymore—you're a leader. If you spark a riot, we all burn."

He was right. The entire Islamic community came running to defend me. But he pulled me aside and held it down. We kept the peace. Days later, the attackers were removed from the unit. I stayed.

Some asked me why I defended the white boy. My answer was simple: "I wasn't defending a white boy. I was defending a human being who couldn't defend himself."

That moment defined my leadership. And it taught me that power isn't always shown through force. Sometimes, power is restraint.

Kendric eventually left the unit. But he left me with everything I needed to lead. Darius's words echoed in my mind: God doesn't place a burden on you greater than what you can bear.

I carried the weight with honor. I led with compassion, truth, and conviction. And when temptation came in the form of a beautiful kitchen worker named Miss T, I almost lost focus. But I pulled back, prayed, and remembered my purpose.

My hard work in the kitchen had shaved 2 years off my mandatory 7 year sentence. When my release day came, I walked out of those gates a free man.

I stepped back into the world no longer defined by my past, but by my growth.

I wasn't just free—I was finally free within myself.

True freedom.

Chapter 12

FREEDOM JANUARY 1998

January 1998. I was 27 years old, and after nearly five years of incarceration, the day I had dreamed of was finally here. It stood in front of me like a light after a long, dark tunnel. I was wearing white kitchen clothes and a pair of battered construction boots—my final prison uniform. In my pocket was a fifty-dollar check from the Department of Corrections, the same issued to every released inmate. That was all I had to my name.

As I stepped through the gates of Neuse Correctional Facility, I saw Omar waiting for me. His face broke into a smile that stretched across years of loyalty. We embraced hard. No words—just brotherhood. Then we jumped in the car and pulled off, with no intention of ever coming back.

The night before, I called him to make sure he was still coming to get me. "I got you, bro," he said. Simple, solid. That's what our bond was built on.

We weren't just friends—we were family. Our mothers, Miss Bess and mine, were close like sisters. I remembered how both of them used to work in the tobacco fields every summer while we were on school break, just to make sure we had snacks and food. My mother would come home filthy, hands crusted with dirt, her skin burnt deep by the sun. Some days, she barely made $28 for eight hours of back-breaking work. But she never complained. Her focus was on our well-being, her love expressed through pain and sacrifice. She'd shower, send us to the store for a Pepsi, and collapse from exhaustion. I never realized then what those sacrifices meant. But during those long, reflective prison nights, I finally understood—and it made me determined to change.

Back in the car, Omar cracked jokes about my prison getup, laughing at my oversized kitchen clothes and dusty boots. But he wasn't clowning me. He was celebrating. "Don't trip," he said, "I'm taking you shopping."

After we picked up Rondo and Brad, we headed straight to Crabtree Valley Mall in Raleigh. It felt surreal. They each handed me cash - $3,000 in pocket money. No questions, no strings. They were just happy to see me home. I left that mall with armfuls of FUBU, Mecca, Phat Farm—gear I used to dream about. LL Cool J had made FUBU iconic, and now it was mine. My brothers made sure I had the freshest Timberlands and Jordans, too. That moment... I felt like I had finally rejoined the world.

But the streets had changed. Hustling was at an all-time high, and word was that my crew was raking in serious dough. People kept telling me, "Yo, your team's getting it. They're gonna bless you." But I had already decided that I wasn't going back to the streets. My conversion to Islam had shifted my thinking. And on top of that, Karen wanted me to come back to Phoenix and work things out. So, after just three days home, I left.

I spent those last days visiting my sisters, my mother, and everyone who held me down. Gigi threw me a welcome-home cookout that meant everything to me. Before my flight, Sarah and I sat up late, laughing about old times. The next day, she rode the bus with me to the airport. Four hours later, I landed in Phoenix. And there she was—Karen—smiling wide like she hadn't ghosted me for years. But I let that go because now here we were. After five years of being told when to eat, sleep, and breathe, I just wanted peace, purpose... and freedom.

My first priority was work. Having my freedom back was cool, but being broke was not. I hit every temp agency and scanned the newspaper for job openings. I thought I could pick up where I left off. But now, I was a felon, stamped with a violent crime. I had taken interview prep classes in prison, but they didn't prepare me for rejection. "We can't hire you because of your past record," they all said.

I started lying on applications out of frustration and finally landed a job at a furniture store. Two months later, I got a call two hours before my shift—fired because my background check came back.

Still, I didn't let it break me.

One day, Karen and I passed a high-rise construction site. I told her to stop the car. I walked straight into the trailer and met the superintendent. He said they weren't hiring, but introduced me to Marcus, the concrete project manager. Marcus hired me on the spot.

A week later, I was clocking in. Karen and I bought work clothes, boots, and tools: a hammer, a cutter, a belt, and a harness. It was grueling work— twelve-hour days in brutal heat. Sometimes I had to come back at 11:30 PM for night pours. I thought prison weightlifting made me strong, but this was different. That concrete vibrator broke my body down. Every muscle ached. Still, I pushed through. Because for once, I was earning it.

But the long hours took a toll on my relationship with Karen. I'd come home, eat, and sleep. That was our routine. We'd fight about money, effort, and dreams. I felt she wasn't pulling her weight. She thought I was being unfair. Eventually, I snapped. I called my boys in North Carolina. The next day, Rondo, Brad, and Omar wired me money and bought me a bus ticket.

I gave Marcus my notice. He understood and wished me well.

But I didn't tell Karen I was leaving.

I waited until she ran errands, packed my bags, called a cab, and headed to the station. As I was boarding, I heard tires screech. Karen had found me. She came flying out of the car—yelling, slapping, tearing my shirt, trying to pull my bag away. I held on. She screamed and cried, but eventually let go.

The whole bus was silent.

Some whispered I was a coward. I sat there, licking my wounds, and closed my eyes. I had three long days to reflect. I was broke. I was homeless. I was headed back to the projects, back to Gigi.

Gigi didn't ask questions. She just opened her door.

But I was hurting. My luggage got lost in Dallas. I had nothing. All my friends were up—getting money, living large. I had pride and faith, but I was tired.

Brad knew. He said, "I got you. I know you ain't on that crack game no more—but you can move some weed."

I thought about it hard. Gigi saw my struggle. Even she said, "You'd make good money, all your boys are."

Eventually, I gave in. Brad bought me two pounds. I didn't start with nickel bags. I went straight to quarter bags and ounces. My crew trained me—taught me how to move smart, who to avoid. I went from two pounds to five in a week. People hated how fast I came up, but it was inevitable. My squad had the streets locked.

We ran Green Acres. Nobody moved without our say-so. Out-of-towners weren't allowed. Our code was loyalty. No reckless talk. Phones got dumped if we heard clicks. I sold weed, not crack—I couldn't go back to destroying lives.

Six months in, I leveled up—started buying hydroponics from Brooklyn. I paid $1,500 per pound and flipped it for $11,200. I introduced Goldsboro to "caskets"—clear containers that preserved quality. I opened a weed spot on the North End. It boomed.

Brooklyn became my second home. I picked up ecstasy pills for $5 and sold them for $25. They flew. Fast money. Big money. But my soul was crumbling. I stopped praying. Lust took over. The fashion, the women—it had me. I had everything I thought I wanted.

Then Gigi opened a liquor store. Legendary. $6,000 in two days selling chicken sandwiches and Hennessy. I ran a card game in the back. It was a feeding ground for women, money, and networking. Gigi was the glue of the city—everyone loved her.

When I decided to start a record label, my boys backed me without hesitation. Omar bought the equipment. We built a studio. We signed an artist. We had momentum—until 9/11 hit.

Everything stopped. No more shipments. No more connections. The price of a key jumped to $30K. Hydro dried up. My studio drained my pockets. I was barely surviving.

So I humbled myself and got a job at a bakery. I kept a little weed hustle on the side. But I had insurance and stability. I was simply surviving.

While others went broke, I stayed afloat.

Later, Gigi loaned me $1,000 from her tax return. I hit the Garment District, bought fashion, and flipped it into $5,000. I opened a women's clothing store, but it wasn't enough. Rent…. Inventory…. Bills…. I was drowning again.

Then Karen called out of nowhere. I told her everything.

The next day, a FedEx package arrived—$1,500 and a note: "Handle your business." I cried. We talked every day, but the store was dying. Someone jealous even threw a brick through my window.

Karen sent a ticket and Gigi helped me shut it down. It was time to go.

Goldsboro had changed. My reputation meant nothing. Gangs ran the streets. My era was over. The brick, the drought, the fatigue—it all screamed one thing: Leave.

So I did.

Chapter 13

BACK TO PHOENIX

In September 2003, I was 32 years old when I returned to Phoenix, carrying the weight of failure but also a flicker of hope. I had just emptied out my clothing store in Goldsboro. I packed up the last of my unsold merchandise in silence and disappeared without saying a word to my landlord. I hated doing it, but I felt I had no other choice. I was drowning in debt, surrounded by betrayal, and burnt out from trying to make something work that no longer could. On that flight to Phoenix, I sat by the window and stared out into the clouds, lost in thought.

I reflected on everything—where I went wrong, what I could have done better, the people who supported me, and those who disappeared when I needed them most. I had poured my heart into that business, but sometimes hard work and passion aren't enough. The economy was shifting. The streets were changing. I was changing. And deep down, I knew it was time for a new chapter.

Returning to Phoenix wasn't just a relocation—it was a homecoming. It was me stepping back into a place where I once had dreams, a place where I had left things unresolved. But this time, I was different. This time, I came back with a plan, a clearer mind, and a willingness to rebuild brick by brick.

When Karen picked me up from the airport, she smiled and hugged me tightly. That one gesture meant the world to me. There were no bitter words, no grudges, no distance. Just a silent understanding that we both wanted to move forward. I knew I had caused pain when I left the way I did the first time around. But now, I was here to make it right, not with empty promises but with action.

The very next day, I hit the pavement running. I woke up early, showered, dressed in my best clothes and went to every temp agency in Phoenix. I filled out applications, went through background checks, and checked every classified ad I could find in the Arizona Republic. I said yes to every opportunity that came my way. Telemarketing jobs that made my head hurt. Graveyard shifts at supply companies that built lawnmower parts—jobs that broke my back and tested my will. But I showed up every day on time. I was hungry and determined.

Eventually, I got a call from a temp agency about a job that paid better. It was temporary, but it was something. I showed up early, not knowing what I would be doing. The receptionist smiled politely and told me to have a seat. I waited in that chair, tapping my foot, trying to steady my nerves. That's when Dave walked in.

He was a short, stocky white guy with kind eyes and a calm demeanor. He introduced himself as the Production Manager at R-Global Aviation and shook my hand like he meant it. We walked the shop floor as he explained what the company did—manufacturing, packing, shipping aviation equipment for military and commercial use. There was an energy in the air, a sense of purpose I hadn't felt in a long time.

Dave introduced me to everyone, then assigned me to a lead named Rex. My job was simple: build shipping crates, paint components, and help wherever I was needed. The tasks were physical, repetitive, and at times exhausting. But I didn't care. I needed this. I wanted this. I gave it everything I had. I stayed late, showed up early, volunteered for the jobs nobody else wanted— emptying trash cans, organizing tools, cleaning up behind others.

R-Global Aviation was a different kind of place. They treated employees like people, not numbers. They gave us free snacks, sodas, coffee, and bagels every Friday. And if you stayed after hours, they fed you. Saturdays were my favorite. J.R., one of the owners, would walk through every department and personally hand every employee a $20 bill, just to say thank you.

What was supposed to be a three-month assignment turned into six. One day, Dave called me into his office. I thought it was over. Instead, he offered me a full-time job—$28,000 a year with full benefits. I couldn't believe it. I shook his hand with tears welling up in my eyes. I walked out of that office and called Karen to tell her the news. She screamed with joy. That night, we celebrated with pancakes and eggs at Denny's. It wasn't fancy, but it felt like we were winning.

My first full-time role was as the go-to guy. I didn't have a title—I just handled errands, deliveries, and supply runs. But I watched, listened, and learned. I asked every lead about their department, the products, and the process. And they took the time to teach me. Dave saw my curiosity and work ethic and created a Facility Maintenance position just for me.

When the company expanded and purchased a new building, Dave put me in charge of the entire move. I was responsible for managing two temporary employees and coordinating with every department. For two weeks, we loaded trucks, set up racks, waxed floors, and rebuilt workspaces. We worked long hours—sometimes from sunrise until midnight. And when it was done, we were spent.

Then, one afternoon, the entire production team was called into the conference room. I expected a rundown about productivity or new safety protocols. But instead, the owners, J.R and H.R., handed out envelopes. I opened mine and nearly dropped it. Inside was a $10,000 bonus check and a note that read, "Thanks for all the hard work, Lawyer."

I was speechless.

Normally, I would've gone home and shared that moment with Karen. But things were changing. We weren't spending much time together. I was working long hours and pouring myself into this new life, and somewhere in the process, we began to drift. I didn't notice it at first. But over time, the conversations got shorter. The connection faded. Eventually, we ended things. Quietly. Sadly.

I moved into a two-bedroom apartment that became my healing space. I rarely left unless it was for work or to help Axis, a local rapper I had started managing. He had raw talent and big dreams, and I saw something in him that reminded me of myself. We poured everything into his music—mixtapes, flyers, press kits, showcases. He got a break when MTV MADE featured him as a coach for a young aspiring rapper. After that, the phone started ringing.

Axis appeared in major hip-hop magazines and collaborated with big DJs. But then the industry crashed. The labels shut down. Deals dried up. We kept releasing music, but no one was listening. And at the same time, the economy collapsed. The housing market crashed. R-Global cut overtime, raises, and bonuses. Money got tight fast.

I took a second job as an assistant manager at Subway just to stay afloat. I worked late nights and weekends, made sandwiches, cleaned floors, managed shifts, and rang up customers with a smile—even when I was exhausted. They fed me every shift and let me take home cookies at closing. I devoured those cookies like they were gourmet meals. Subway was a blessing—it kept groceries in my fridge and dignity in my heart.

Through all of this, I never stopped grinding. Never stopped believing. I knew the struggle intimately. I knew what it was like to go without. But I also knew how to survive. And I was determined not to go backward.

Then came comedy. Comedy didn't just help me laugh—it helped me heal. It gave me courage. It gave me a voice. It gave me the strength to stop hiding my past and face it head-on in front of the world. For the first time in my life, I could speak openly about my trauma—the childhood abuse, the incarceration, the pain of being silenced for years—and do it in a way that gave others the freedom to laugh, feel, and relate.

Comedy allowed me to show my vulnerabilities. To let go of shame. To say, "This happened to me, but it was not my fault." I was just a child. A child who didn't deserve what happened. A child who had to learn how to survive before he even learned how to live. Every punchline was a piece of pain released. Every set was a session of therapy. It became my relief, my medicine, my way to feel better about myself.

Inspired by Richard Pryor and Eddie Murphy— and sharpened by years of snapping jokes in the streets—I wrote material every day. I studied YouTube, read books, and analyzed performances. Three months in, I hit the stage at Stand Up Scottsdale. I was terrified. But once the lights hit my face, everything else disappeared. People laughed. I got addicted to the feeling.

Week after week, I got better. Then, one night, I bombed. Bad. I stood on that stage and watched a room full of people stare back at me in silence. I wanted to quit, but I couldn't. A veteran comic named D.W. pulled me aside and said, "Stop talking at them. Talk to them. Be real."

He was right. I adjusted, improved, and grew. I didn't follow cliques. I built my own lane. I promoted myself like I had done with Axis—flyers, Facebook, and tagging everyone. Some comics hated it and told me to slow down. They said I was being too flashy. I didn't care. I was making noise.

Axis came on board as my manager. I booked bigger shows—Phoenix, L.A., Atlanta, Texas, Colorado. My first big L.A. performance was humbling. I bombed again. But I went back to work—studying Def Comedy Jam, rewriting material, getting sharper. Six months later, I returned and killed it. That night, I got invited back.

R-Global helped me buy my first home. I walked through each room, thanking God. I was the first in my family to own a home. And it all started with one pair of pants and a heart full of hustle.

Ms. G., the company's secretary, and Ms. J., the office manager, were my guardian angels at R-Global. They protected me, defended me, and encouraged me. When collectors called the job, they handled it. When people mistreated me, they went to management. They were my family. Without them, life at R-Global could have been miserable. With them, it became a place of growth, love, and protection.

When J.R. passed away, it was like a piece of the company's soul disappeared. His absence was heavy. People walked around quietly. We still worked, but the heart wasn't the same. Then, ten years later, Ms. J passed too. When I found out, I was shattered. Her office was being cleared out on a Monday morning. My manager pulled me aside

and said, "Ms. J. passed away over the weekend."
I sat in my office in complete shock. A thick silence
settled across the company like a fog. It was a pain
you couldn't describe, a thickness in the air that
couldn't be measured. With Ms. J's passing, a part
of me went with her. After J.R. passed, the
company leadership was passed down to Blair, a
retired Colonel in the U.S. Army. Blair carried
himself with the same grace and integrity that J.R.
had. He was a leader who greeted everyone by
name, walked the production floor daily, and
made every employee—from the janitor to the
project managers—feel like they mattered. Blair led
with discipline, but also compassion. He secured
contracts that kept us busy for years. Under his
leadership, the company held on to the values J.R.
instilled—respect, transparency, and loyalty.
Working under Blair felt like you were still part of
J.R.'s original vision. He was that kind of leader.
Steady. Firm. Fair.

But everything changed when Blair retired and
new leadership stepped in. The heart of the
company faded. The culture that once united us
slowly began to unravel. New management didn't

carry the same warmth or integrity. People started choosing sides. The workplace felt colder and you could feel the shift in energy. It wasn't just a change in structure—it was a loss of spirit.

Then one day, a coworker posted a noose on his whiteboard, mocking the Bubba Wallace incident. He laughed it off and said we were "too sensitive." He claimed being Chilean was harder than being Black. I was livid and had to go to the break room to cool off. I never looked at him the same. That moment changed me. I wanted to speak the truth. I started a podcast—The Lawyer Johnson Talk Radio Show. Every Saturday at 1 p.m., I interviewed real people—realtors, activists, comedians. I fundraised for youth teams. And through that podcast, I met Daisy. The woman who would become my wife and my partner in healing.

Sometimes, the deepest pain leads you to the most unexpected joy. And sometimes, the ugliest chapters birth the most beautiful new beginnings

Chapter 14

DAISY

Daisy and I met in one of the most unexpected ways—through Facebook. At the time, I was traveling across the country doing stand-up comedy, building up my podcast, and staying focused on my grind. I had no clue who she was when she sent me a friend request. I accepted it without thinking much—maybe she was a fan of the podcast or my stand-up, I figured. But then, everything changed.

A comedian friend of mine reached out, asking if I could help promote a show he was doing at the House of Comedy in Phoenix. I agreed and sent out invites offering free tickets to all my Facebook friends—Daisy included. She showed up. That night, we crossed paths briefly in the lobby after the show. I was there with a date and some friends, so our interaction was short. Just a smile, a hello, and then we went our separate ways.

A few days later, Daisy messaged me again—not for herself, but to ask if I could promote a fundraiser for her son's football team on my podcast. I respected that she came with a purpose, not a flirt. I agreed immediately and invited her and her son onto the show. We talked about her son's accomplishments, what position he played, and the goals for his team. That's where our friendship started.

After the recording, I walked her to her car. She handed me a small bundt cake and a thank-you card. It was simple, heartfelt, and incredibly thoughtful. Nothing flashy—just a woman showing gratitude in the most sincere way. That gesture stuck with me.

Soon after, Daisy invited me to her home for dinner because her son had bragged during the interview how his mom was a great cook. At first, I didn't want to go. I had already made a promise to myself: no more dating, no distractions, no pouring into people who didn't pour back. Six months before meeting Daisy, I was in a short-lived relationship that left me emotionally exhausted.

Since then, I stayed focused, locked in on my comedy, my talk show, and my healing. But something in me told me to accept her invitation.

When I pulled up to her house, I was stunned. It was big, clean, and felt like something out of a luxury magazine. The landscaping was immaculate, and as soon as I walked in, the smell of salmon, potatoes, and asparagus filled the air. Her kitchen was spotless. There was a fully stocked drink fridge, a beautiful coffee bar, and a liquor bar that could compete with any five-star restaurant. Her kids greeted me warmly. They made me feel welcome.

After dinner, Daisy gave me a tour of her home— there was a pool, basketball court, trampoline, outdoor kitchen, and flat-screen TV mounted on the patio. It was clear: she had built something beautiful for her family, and I respected every part of it. Still, I kept my boundaries. I wasn't there to chase anything. She didn't make me feel pressured either. When her car battery died, she asked for help. I came, she made dinner, I ate, and I left. No games. Just friendship.

One afternoon, while we were eating sushi near my job, she looked at me and asked, "Why aren't you dating anyone?" That caught me off guard. I told her the truth—I didn't trust people anymore. I was afraid of falling in love again and getting hurt. I wasn't ready.

I needed someone who matched my energy, someone who didn't just take from my spirit and leave me running on fumes.

When I told Daisy that, she didn't try to convince me otherwise. She gave me space. She respected my boundaries. She just kept showing up. I stayed focused, stayed disciplined—and then Daisy showed up in my life in a way I never expected.

She wasn't just a good woman—she was a powerful woman. A dentist with her own practice, a homeowner, two fully paid vehicles, and a heart that didn't need anything from me except the truth. But honestly? None of her material accomplishments moved me. What got me was her spirit, her humility, her peace. I wasn't looking for a relationship, but somehow, I was walking right into the arms of something real.

When I planned a trip to Italy, Daisy offered to take me to the airport. She picked me up, helped pack my bags, and dropped me off. While I was away, we spoke often. Nine days in Rome, and she never once made me feel pressured or tied down. I came back and brought her wine and gifts, and found myself thinking about her more than I expected.

About six months into our friendship, she looked me in the eye and said, "You need to give love a chance again. Stop being afraid. I'm not here to hurt you." Her words hit me deep. That night, I prayed to God. "If she's the one, show me a sign."

Soon after, she called me crying. Her father was in the hospital, and she didn't know if he was going to make it. Out of everyone in her life, she called me. I sat with her on the phone as she wept—and in that moment, I knew. That was my sign.

From there, we moved forward. I made the decision to move in with her, and I listed my townhouse on Airbnb for supplemental income. Living with her felt natural, but I was still navigating old wounds. Daisy never judged me. When things got tough, she suggested counseling—not to fix me, but to understand me better. I told her about my past—how I went to prison for armed robbery, how I carried a felony. She didn't flinch. "You're not that man anymore," she said. "You've evolved."

We were both Pisces, both shaped by bad relationships. She had three kids from a previous marriage. I had six-two before prison, and four after. I already had four grandchildren when we met, and I told her plainly: my grandchildren are my world. Daisy embraced them like they were her own, building bonds with each of them, with no hesitation.

At that point, my finances were all over the place. Daisy sat me down, taught me how to budget, and helped me create order. I gave her full transparency because I respected her. I was always taught to be honest and give people a choice before asking them to build a life with you.

Two years later, I made the choice to sell my townhouse. I used the money to pay off my debt and buy Daisy an engagement ring. She said it was too expensive, but to me, it was just a reflection of how much she meant to me. I wasn't just investing in a ring—I was investing in our future.

Before we got married, I made another big decision: I retired from R-Global Aviation after 18 years. The truth was, the company didn't value me. Every year, I had to fight for a raise, and every year my requests were denied. Daisy saw my potential. She encouraged me to step out on faith. "Start your own business. You deserve to be in control of your future."

So I did it. I studied, passed my exams, and launched my construction company. I gave my manager a one-month notice. When my last day arrived, they threw a retirement party. I was handed a plaque, a cake, and a room full of farewells. Even the head of HR asked if someone had wronged me. I told her the truth—I just needed something new. I needed to grow.

One person who stood by me throughout was M.R., a supervisor in another department and a retired Air Force Master Sergeant. He was like a big brother, teaching me how to evolve from the street mentality to a professional mindset. "You have to follow before you lead," he'd say. He was the only one who knew I was retiring before it happened. Losing that daily connection hurt the most.

After retirement, I joined a business group through my realtor. Within a week, I landed a $30,000 renovation job in Scottsdale. I did the entire project myself. When I finished, the owner gave me a $2,000 bonus. It took a toll on my body, but it confirmed my purpose.

Then came the biggest job yet: a $200,000 project converting a monastery school into a doggie daycare. What should've been a three-month job turned into eight due to delays with permits and an architect who got fired and rehired mid-project. I spent more time fixing building plans than swinging a hammer. When the city finally approved everything, we pushed through. New plumbing, masonry, electrical, landscaping—it was done. I earned the certificate of occupancy and peace of mind.

Daisy never left my side. When I got sick, she ran her dental practice and the construction business. She managed schedules, ordered materials, and even unloaded boxes of tile. She didn't complain—she executed.

When we got married on March 11, 2022, Daisy planned everything herself: the DJ, the tables, the food, the chairs, the backyard décor. Our families came from all over. We laughed, danced, celebrated—and everything came full circle.

Daisy is my answered prayer. She loves me deeply and accepts every part of who I am. She helped me grow from a man still healing into a man thriving.

A friend once told me, "When the right woman comes along, you won't have to chase her. She'll be right in front of you."

And he was right.

Chapter 15

BREAKING THE SILENCE

It was a beautiful summer morning, and I was outside playing with my Hot Wheels cars in front of our building. Out of nowhere, my next-door neighbor, Deon, offered me some cookies. He was a family friend, someone I trusted, so I didn't hesitate when he encouraged me to come down into his basement to get them. But what seemed like a harmless invitation turned out to be a trap. In that basement, Deon sexually abused me.

I tried to fight back. I screamed for help, but he overpowered me. Afterward, he threatened me into silence. I walked home numb, in shock. I was only seven years old, and I couldn't comprehend what had just happened.

When I reached home, shame and disgust washed over me. I thought I had done something wrong. I believed I had let my mother down and that she would be mad at me. So, I buried it. For forty plus years, I carried that secret.

I never imagined Deon would betray me like that. He wasn't just a neighbor—he was my sister Gigi's best friend's uncle. The betrayal felt personal, deep. The freedom and joy I once found in playing outside vanished that day. I no longer trusted anyone, especially adult men—except for my uncles. I lived with a protective force field around me every day.

When another one of Deon's friends tried to approach me in the same way, I ran for my life. After that, I stayed glued to my mother's side. I wouldn't go outside without her watching me. The joyful, carefree part of me died. My awareness became heightened. I wanted to tell my mother, but I was terrified. I hated Deon. I wish I'd been old enough to fight him off. He stole a part of me I could never get back. The trauma he inflicted on me became a scar on my soul.

For most of my life, I lived in fight, flight, or freeze mode. That moment played on repeat in my mind. I never understood the root of my mental health struggles until I started researching how trauma—poverty, death, and especially sexual abuse—can shape a person's mind. I traced my anger issues, trust problems, recklessness—all of it—back to that basement.

It wasn't until Desiree, my friend and motivational speaking coach, encouraged me to dig deep into my own story that I truly began to understand. She wanted me to be fully prepared to speak on adversity. That meant going back to my own darkness. I always wanted to help young people transition out of trauma. But I knew I couldn't help others unless I gave them 100% of my truth.

Comedy became my tool to open up in front of crowds. My life, every trial and lesson, was preparing me to connect with other survivors. I started volunteering at juvenile detention centers, helping youth shift their mindsets, teaching entrepreneurship.

When I first entered those centers, the teens sized me up like I was nobody. But once I shared my story—five years in prison, facing 200 years after a friend snitched—they listened. I saw myself in them. Some wouldn't go home for a long time. But I asked each of them the same question: "If you could do anything, what would it be?"

They talked about families, marriage, and businesses. That gave me hope. I researched resources—barber schools, trade programs, licensing steps—and gave them information to start mapping out their future. Helping them gave me a sense of peace I'd never known.

But something still weighed on me. I hadn't told my family. I was working on a documentary about my life and didn't want them finding out on film. I had to tell them myself.

Just the thought of it brought back the fear. My emotional defense—"the switch"—would kick in every time the memory of Deon surfaced. That switch, which helped me survive as a child, now kept me from healing. It shut down the words before they could escape.

Breaking that silence took more courage than anything I faced in prison. There wasn't a dramatic moment that led to it—just years of pain becoming too heavy to carry. I was finally ready to reclaim my life.

It was time to call my sisters. I sat alone, rehearsing my words. My heart raced, my palms sweaty. My body thought it was under attack. That's how deeply my fear had rooted.

When I finally called them, I told them everything. The phone fell silent. It was a silence louder than words.

Gigi finally broke it. "You lived with that all this time and never told anyone?" Her voice cracked. It hit me like a punch. She was shaken. My strong big sister was shattered by my news.

She kept asking why I never told her or Mom. I could hear the pain, the disbelief. And then she shared something I never expected—her own story. Similar to me, she also kept silent.

She opened up, even in her pain, to protect me. To show me I wasn't alone. That moment built a deeper bond between us.

Sarah's reaction was fierce. She was furious. She wanted to destroy Deon. She said if she had known, she would've gone to war. That's who she was—loud, blunt, fearless.

I remember when someone broke into her house and stole her furniture. She found the girl and beat her so badly that she needed stitches. Sarah didn't play. She asked me how I had survived with that secret. I told her I was scared. Scared Deon would hurt them or me if I told anyone.

Her rage was what I should've had as a child— protection, fury, love. But it also made me wonder how different things could have been had I spoken sooner.

Sarah told me I needed to tell Mom. And she stood by me.

A year later, during Mom's 70th birthday weekend in North Carolina, Sarah and I sat down with her.

"Mom, I need to tell you something," I began. "Something that happened when I was little."

She looked puzzled. As I spoke, I saw her shift. She went quiet. "What?" she asked. Then stared into space. "I always knew something was different about that boy."

She didn't cry. But I saw it in her face. Her silence said everything.

My mother, who rarely showed emotion, was broken. Her eyes glazed over. Her hands—those hard-working, sacrifice-worn hands—clutched the chair like she was holding herself together.

She mentally revisited our life in Newburgh, every moment she may have missed. I could see it all flashing through her eyes.

She didn't need to say much. I felt her heartbreak. And in that silence, something lifted inside me.

In the weeks after, my relationship with my sisters changed. There was more understanding. Less tension. They saw parts of me they hadn't understood before. And I felt freer.

I had lived in two versions of myself: the tough Lawyer Johnson the world knew, and the wounded seven-year-old boy inside. Those versions were always at war. That war shaped everything—my relationships, my reactions. I was exhausted from living a divided life.

God was speaking to me, telling me to become an open book. For once, it wasn't about me. It was about saving lives. But first, I had to break out of the mental prison Deon had built.

I recorded a video sharing my transformational journey—and the childhood abuse I'd hidden for decades. I posted it on social media. For a moment, I felt fear—what would people think? But it quickly passed. This wasn't about me.

Within hours, I felt a strange peace. The wall of pain I'd hidden behind began to fall. For the first time, I felt like I was living my purpose. My hardships, once heavy burdens, became tools to help others rebuild their lives. I began to see adversity not as a curse, but as a blessing. Because without defeat, how do you learn how to overcome?

But the biggest shift was internal. Speaking my truth helped me reclaim lost parts of myself. Pieces I'd hidden, buried.

Others began opening up. Friends, strangers—they told me their own stories of trauma. I realized I wasn't alone. What was rare wasn't the abuse—it was the honesty.

Breaking my silence wasn't just about telling others. It was about finally telling myself the truth that I had survived. That I was worthy. That my pain didn't define me.

And even now, healing isn't linear. Some days, I'm triggered. Some days, I'm back in that basement. But I no longer walk this journey alone. My family, my wife, the people I've helped—they walk it with me.

In the end, I found my voice.

But there's one piece still missing. One that's been with me since childhood.

Who is my father?

For fifty years, I had lived without that answer. My mom never gave it to me. Uncle W. filled the role beautifully. But now that I've faced my past, maybe it's time I faced this, too. Maybe it's time I found out where I really came from—and why he was never there.

Chapter 16

FINDING MY FATHER

For fifty years, I lived with a void—a missing piece of my identity. I always wondered who my father was. Every now and then, I'd muster the courage to ask my mother, hoping for a name, a clue, anything. But she never gave me a straight answer. Eventually, I stopped asking. I buried the ache and tried to fill that emptiness in other ways.

Fortunately, my Uncle W. stepped in and became the man I needed. He didn't just play a role—he lived it. Uncle W. raised me like a son, guided me with strength, and showed me what a man was supposed to be. He was steady, firm, and loving in his own way. When he passed away in 2015, I was devastated. At his funeral, as I stared at him resting in his crisp three-piece suit, and polished Florsheim shoes, I realized just how much he had meant to me. I quietly thanked him for shaping me, for being there when no one else was.

I told him I was finally doing well. That I was working a good job, getting my life together. But nothing prepared me for the weight of seeing him gone. He was more than just family—he was my foundation.

He never judged me for my mistakes. When I came home from Rikers Island, lost and uncertain, he didn't question me. He simply asked, "You okay? So what's your plan now?" That was his way— always forward-thinking. When I didn't want to go to school and claimed I had no bus fare, he made sure I had some. No excuses. Just solutions.

He got me up every Saturday morning to clean the apartment. I'd mop, sweep, and dust before running to the store with a list of groceries. Only after completing my chores was I allowed to hang out. Uncle W. believed in discipline, structure, and responsibility. "If you're not doing the right thing, don't make excuses," he'd tell me. "Own your actions. Try harder until you figure it out." Those words still live inside me.

Despite everything my uncle gave me, there was still a quiet void. A piece of me still longed for something more—a deeper truth I couldn't ignore forever.

Years earlier, my cousin Tanisha told me about a DNA service that helped her find relatives she never knew existed. She encouraged me to try it. At first, I was hesitant. What if the truth was painful? What if he was already gone? What if he knew about me and never cared?

Even Daisy suggested hiring a private investigator, but I dismissed it. I wasn't ready to dig into a past that might break me all over again. I told myself I had made it this far without him.

But curiosity crept in.

I first took a DNA test through African Ancestry to discover my ethnic background. I wanted to know where my people came from, what tribe I belonged to. The results awakened something in me. I needed more. I signed up for Ancestry.com, swabbed my mouth, and waited.

For 45 days, I checked that dashboard like clockwork. When the results came in, most of the connections were on my mother's side—names from New York and North Carolina. Then I started seeing relatives in South Carolina. A few third cousins popped up with DNA matches around 5%. Tanisha, my closest maternal cousin, was 13%.

But then—someone new: Adam. He was a 14% match. Higher than Tanisha. The catch? I had never heard of Adam. Could he be from my father's side?

I reached out and explained that I was searching for my biological father. Adam responded instantly and was eager to help. I gave him my mother's name and where I was born. He got back to me the next day and said, "I think my uncle Gilbert might be your father."

Gilbert Smith. He had lived in Newburgh for fifty years—my hometown. He had recently retired and moved to Atlanta. Adam told me that despite being eighty-five years old he was still sharp and active.

Adam gave me his number and wished me luck.

I was terrified. I stared at that number for two weeks. Fear of rejection kept me frozen. What if he didn't want to be found?

Daisy pushed me again. "Stop being negative," she said. "Just call him."

I finally did.

The call went to voicemail. I left a short message and hung up, heart pounding. Three hours later, my phone rang. It was Gilbert.

His voice came through the line: "How can I help you, and who are you supposed to be to me?"

I took a breath. "According to my DNA match with your nephew Adam… it looks like you might be my father."

He paused. "You've got to be kidding me," he said. "Well… I respect your courage to reach out. I'll call you back in a couple of days."

Click.

I felt gutted. Empty. Like I had walked into a door I wasn't supposed to open.

For two days, I battled with every emotion. Daisy noticed the shift in me and called her mother because she knew her advice would help. Ann's words grounded me: "He's 80-something. You don't know what kind of life he's living. That kind of news is shocking. Give him time."

And she was right. Gilbert called back that Saturday morning.

Before anything else, I told him I wasn't looking to blame or disrupt his life. I just wanted to get to know him. I only wanted a father-son relationship—nothing more.

We talked for ten minutes. He was calm, curious, and respectful. He promised to call every weekend. And he did.

Daisy, overjoyed, booked flights to Atlanta. I picked up another DNA test kit to confirm everything.

We arranged to meet Gilbert at a restaurant called Paschal's —a well-known Atlanta spot. When we arrived, Gilbert was already there, seated at a table near the window. I watched him glance outside, nervously fidgeting like a kid waiting for his family to show up.

As we walked in, he stood and opened his arms wide. He hugged Daisy, the kids, and then me. It was warm, heartfelt—like he had been waiting a long time for that moment.

Lisa, his adopted daughter, joined us and helped coordinate everything. She picked the restaurant and shared its history with us. Once seated, we ordered: I got fried catfish, collard greens, potato salad, and cornbread. Gilbert went for the fried chicken, and when that food hit the table, he cleaned his plate like he hadn't eaten all day. We laughed. He reminded me of my mother—same appetite, same joy in a good meal.

During that lunch, I didn't need a DNA test to know he was my father. We had the same nose. The same earring in the same ear. The same energy. It was clear. But we still did the test for confirmation.

The result came in: 99.99% match.

Gilbert Smith was my father. However, he never knew I existed until I reached out and called him. Everything finally started making sense.

He told me that if he'd known I was his son back then, nothing would've stopped him from being in my life, not even his wife. But time was gone. I told him, "Let's not focus on the past. Let's make memories now."

And we did.

He came to Arizona for two weeks. We visited the Grand Canyon—he kept calling it "that big hole in the ground," and was completely blown away. When his visit was over, I flew back with him to Atlanta. He introduced me to all his friends. They spoke so highly of him—how he inspired them to walk daily, helped them lose weight, and kept them motivated. I was proud to call him my Dad.

When I started working on my affordable housing blueprint, he was the first person I told. It was the same with earning my electrical and plumbing licenses. When he said, "I'm proud of you," it filled something in me I didn't even know was still empty.

Daisy even surprised him with tickets to the Falcons vs. Cardinals game. He was blown away by how close our seats were—close enough to see the owner and players on the sideline. That day, he was like a kid. It was beautiful.

For the first time in my life, I had a father. I had a name. A face. A history.

But just as I was finding this missing piece, I lost another.

My sister Sarah passed away in September 2024—just nine months before this book was completed.

Sarah was my protector, my soldier. She was loyal to a fault and had more heart than anyone I knew. When I was on the streets, she never judged me. She gave me her welfare checks to flip, helped stock my store, hid money and weapons, gave me gas money, and pawned tools for me. She never asked for more than I could give. She just loved me.

She was the first person I told about Daisy being white. Her response? "The world's past that. Be happy." She had my back in everything.

When I broke out of jail, she fed me and kept me safe. When I was released with nothing, she housed me and rode the bus with me to the airport. She even sent me money after tax season. Sarah always kept her promises.

She was my emergency contact for life. If I could only make one phone call, it would've been to her.

Her death crushed me. Seeing her in that casket... I wasn't ready. My heart broke again when I heard my mother cry out at the funeral, "Why did you have to go before me?" That moment is burned into my soul.

At the funeral, a woman told me, "Sarah always talked about you. You were her world." I smiled through my tears. That was my sister.

I still want to call her. I want to tell her how much this book means. How I finally found my Dad. I want her to brag to everyone that her brother is a New York Times best-selling author.

I can still hear her saying, "Do your thing, little brother!"

And when the grief hits hardest, I whisper to the sky, "Sarah baby, I love you. Come visit me sometime. I still need your guidance."

You were one of a kind.

And I'll carry your spirit with me—forever.

EPILOGUE

As I watch the Arizona sunset paint the sky in beautiful oranges and purples, I reflect on the journey that brought me here. From the housing projects of Goldsboro to the cells of Rikers Island, from breaking out of jail to breaking the generational cycles of trauma—my life has been anything but ordinary.

The seven-year-old boy who lost his innocence in that basement has traveled a long road to become the man I am today. That violation changed my trajectory, setting me on a path of anger, distrust, and self-destruction. For decades, I carried that burden alone, letting it shape my decisions in ways I didn't fully understand until I found the courage to confront it.

I've worn many faces throughout my life: the scared child, the defiant teenager, the hustler, the fugitive, the inmate, the comedian, the businessman. Each one searching for something— respect, freedom, validation, or purpose. What I've come to understand is that healing doesn't come from escaping the pain but from facing it head-on.

Even now, I'm still learning. That early trauma rewired my brain. My nervous system remains on high alert. I still don't like people standing behind me. Large crowds unsettle me. I constantly scan my surroundings when children are playing. The need to protect never turns off, not just for my grandchildren but for every child I see.

Just recently, during a trip to New York with my wife, we walked through Times Square and I caught myself gripping her hand tightly, unable to relax. She kept whispering, "It's okay, baby. You're safe." And I tried to believe her, to surrender to the moment. But the paranoia didn't let go.

That old internal switch, my survival mode, has served me well. It helped me stay alive in dangerous places. But now I'm learning to control it, to tell the difference between real threats and shadows from the past. Healing isn't about turning off the switch—it's about retraining it. Teaching it to serve my peace, not my panic.

For years, I poured my pain into hustling, comedy, and constant movement—always searching for peace but afraid to sit still. It wasn't until I chose to face my trauma and use it for something bigger that I started to heal.

That decision birthed Motivational Wingz.

Motivational Wingz began with a simple idea: to give young people the mentorship and opportunities I never had. I started by volunteering at juvenile detention centers, speaking from my heart to kids who reminded me of myself. Tough on the outside, terrified on the inside. Many had never heard anyone say, "I believe in you."

I started telling them my story—not to glorify it, but to show them it's possible to change. That there's a way to channel pain into power, fear into focus. The more I spoke, the more I saw light flicker in their eyes. That flicker is why I built the program.

Motivational Wingz is now a full mentorship and life skills program rooted in four healing pillars: finding yourself, accepting your past, understanding your trauma, and discovering your purpose.

Finding yourself means reconnecting with who you were before the trauma. For me, it meant remembering that bright, imaginative boy who once wanted to be a firefighter.

Accepting your past means acknowledging that what happened wasn't your fault. That your trust issues, your outbursts, your fears—they're not flaws. They're responses to being hurt. Letting go of shame allowed me to grow.

Understanding your trauma means educating yourself—learning how your brain and body respond to fear and betrayal. Once I knew why I flinched when someone stood behind me or why I couldn't handle chaos, I started to reclaim control.

And finding your purpose means reigniting the passions that once brought you joy. For me, comedy became the bridge between pain and healing. It gave me a way to laugh, to breathe, and to connect.

I tell the young men we work with: healing has no age limit. I was in my fifties when I broke my silence. It's never too late to take back your life. Never.

Motivational Wingz isn't just a program. It's a promise that your past doesn't define you. That healing is possible. That your voice matters.

Every time I speak to a survivor, I remind them that once, they had no control. But now, they can choose. They can protect themselves. They can love without fear. The strength that once fueled their survival can now power their growth.

Everything I teach through Motivational Wingz comes from experience, not theory. I lived it. I survived it. And I found purpose in the pain. That's what I offer others—the roadmap I wish someone had given me.

Faith has been my anchor through it all. I believe God doesn't waste pain. He repurposes it. What happened to me wasn't God's doing, but I believe He's using it. Every time I speak the truth, every time I help a young man believe in his worth, I'm fulfilling a purpose bigger than me.

This healing journey hasn't been linear. It's come with new challenges and unexpected gifts. One of those gifts was finding my father late in life. Meeting Gilbert at eighty-five years old helped me reclaim a missing piece of my identity. Our time together has been redemptive, filled with new memories and quiet healing.

And then there's Daisy—my wife, my partner, my peace. She didn't just love me. She walked with me through the wreckage. She changed my diet when my diabetes got out of control, booked us healing trips, and held me through panic attacks. She believed in me when I didn't believe in myself.

Daisy and I come from two different worlds. She was raised on a farm in North Dakota, fishing, hunting, and learning discipline from her father. She became a dentist and built her own practice. I grew up in survival mode, in the streets, figuring life out as I went. But somehow, we found each other. And in our differences, we built something solid.

Now, we run businesses together, laugh often, and live with purpose. She's my partner in love and in healing.

I also think of my lifelong friend, Omar. Our bond runs deeper than friendship—it's brotherhood. Even through his health battles, he never stopped showing up for me. When Sarah passed, he and his mother, Miss Bess, wrapped my family in love. He showed up. He always does.

And Brad—my true brother. The one who stood by me when I hit rock bottom. His love is loud, funny, and always real. We've made memories that still make me laugh out loud.

To my sister Gigi, thank you. You never gave up on me. Through every court date, every prison visit, every holiday when I had nothing, you were there. Your loyalty held me together.

To my mother—you are my hero. You never turned your back on me. You walked miles to care for us, washed my football uniform by hand, cooked when I came home from prison, and sent letters when I was locked away. Your love saved me. You believed when I couldn't.

MY CHILDREN

I want to thank my children, both biological and step, who have witnessed every stage of my evolution — from a father shaped by trauma to a father healing through progress. I wish I could have given you a version of me untouched by pain, unclouded by confusion — a version of me that loved you without the stains of the streets, the weight of poverty, or the misguided toughness I once believed defined fatherhood.

Instead of softness, I often gave you survival. But through it all, your presence, your patience, and your love became my redemption.

Now, as a grandfather, your children have brought me joy and renewed energy. They've taught me the true meaning of unconditional love — the kind that doesn't judge but simply accepts. Because of them, I've learned how to slow down, to truly listen, and to be more present. They value my attention in ways that humble me daily.

To each of you, I say: never live in fear. Be the best version of yourself. Follow your heart, not the voices that say you can't. Live your life freely, and make happiness your own — not a reflection of what others expect of you. Don't bury the person you are to please the world. Be real, be bold, and most importantly, be you.

MY IN-LAWS

I want to thank my in-laws, who reshaped my understanding that love truly comes in many colors. You never judged me by the color of my skin, my past, or my education. Instead, you saw my heart — how I loved your daughter and cared for your grandkids — and that was all that mattered.

When I started my company, you didn't hesitate to support my vision. You put your hands in the pile with me and gave me more than just words of encouragement — you gave me a truck and trailer to get started. But it wasn't just the gift — it was the way you delivered it, driving it all the way from North Dakota with no expectations, no strings attached. Just love, support, and belief in me.

Eugene and Ann, you are truly amazing. Thank you for the countless ways you've shown up for me over the years. Your love has made a lasting impact on my life, and I'll never take it for granted.

MY EXTENDED FAMILY AND R-GLOBAL AVIATION FAMILY

I want to extend my deepest thanks to all my nieces, nephews, cousins, friends, and my R-Global Aviation family. Your love, encouragement, and unwavering support over the years have meant more to me than words can express.

Through every season — the highs and the lows — you've stood by me, believed in me, and reminded me of the strength that comes from having a solid circle. Thank you for being part of my journey and for pouring so much light into my life.

ACKNOWLEDGMENT

Last but certainly not least, I want to express my deepest gratitude to Dr. H.R. You gave me the opportunity to be part of your company, and that changed the course of my life. Today, your nameplate hangs above the door of my office as a daily reminder of the incredible man you were and the lessons you taught me.

I'll never forget the day I asked you what it takes to build something extraordinary. You looked at me and said, "You just have to keep going." Simple words, but they carried the weight of a lifetime of wisdom.

Even though you had wealth and success, you lived with humility. You carried yourself with quiet strength and grace. Whenever something needed to be done around your home, I was honored to be the first person you called—because you trusted me.

Your passing was sudden and left a void in so many hearts. The day we lost you, we didn't just lose a leader; we lost a friend, a mentor, and a giant of a man. Even after you retired, you still made time to stop by and check on me, always showing your support and encouragement.

Thank you, H.R., for believing in me when I didn't always believe in myself. I hope everything I'm building today makes you proud. Rest peacefully, my friend. Your legacy lives on through all of us who were blessed to know you and through the impact you made at R-Global Aviation.

If you're reading this and carrying pain, know this: healing is possible. You are not alone. Your voice matters. When you speak, you light the way for others. When you heal, you help us all heal. You deserve freedom. You deserve peace. And most of all, you deserve love.

This is how we break the cycle—one voice, one truth, one act of courage at a time.

Please visit:

www.lawyerjohnsonmotivationalwingz.com for more information about the author.